DEPENDENCY AND DENIAL

AF631600

ALSO IN THE PSYCHOTHERAPY MATTERS SERIES

Life and Hope Out of Darkness:
Creative Interventions for Helping People in Violent Communities
by Sarah Coleman

Bringing Your Heart to Work:
A Seven-Step Journey to Mental Health and Wellbeing
by Hazel A. Hyslop

Sexual Diversity
by Silva Neves

DEPENDENCY AND DENIAL

The Stories That Divide Us

Joseph Pawson

UKCP
UK Council for Psychotherapy

KARNAC
firing the mind

First published in 2026 by
Karnac Books Limited
62 Bucknell Road
Bicester
Oxfordshire OX26 2DS

Copyright © 2026 Joseph Pawson

The right of Joseph Pawson to be identified as the author of this work has been asserted in accordance with §§ 77 and 78 of the Copyright, Designs and Patents Act 1988.

All rights reserved. No part of this publication may be reproduced, stored in a retrieval system, or transmitted, in any form or by any means, electronic, mechanical, photocopying, recording, or otherwise, without the prior written permission of the publisher.

British Library Cataloguing in Publication Data

A C.I.P. for this book is available from the British Library

ISBN: 978-1-80013-451-5 (paperback)
ISBN: 978-1-80013-453-9 (e-book)
ISBN: 978-1-80013-452-2 (PDF)

Typeset by vPrompt eServices Pvt Ltd, India

www.firingthemind.com

MIX
Paper | Supporting responsible forestry
FSC
www.fsc.org
FSC® C007915

Karnac Books is committed to a sustainable future for our business, our readers, and our planet.
This book is made from Forest Stewardship Council® certified paper.

Contents

Acknowledgements

To the many teachers I have been fortunate enough to have. I hope to reflect some of the gifts you have given me in the pages of this book. You are too many to name, but you know who you are, and I am truly grateful.

Specific thanks to those who have contributed to this book, including Conor for his belief and editing at the early stages. To my mother, Gilly, for the many hours spent editing page by page and for supporting me along the way. To Kate, Linda, and everyone on the publishing team who has helped make this book a reality.

To all my relationships, both supportive and challenging, that have led me towards my vulnerability. In particular, to Dani, who has been patiently alongside me whilst writing. And finally, to my clients, who courageously share their pain, enriching both this book and my life immeasurably.

About the author

Joseph Pawson is an integrative psychotherapist whose work brings together interpersonal and transpersonal approaches. Joe grew up in London, where early encounters with altered states of consciousness led him to Peru to explore traditional shamanic practices. There, his experiences inspired him to study herbal medicine at Westminster University, where he earned a first-class BSc. After three years in private clinical practice, he came to see the symbolic and psychological dimensions of healing as the most powerful aspect of his work. This recognition led him to train in integrative psychotherapy at the Bath Centre for Psychotherapy and Counselling, where he was able to develop the relational and interpersonal side of his practice. At the heart of his work is a trust that the unconscious intelligence latent in the psychotherapy process will unfold in its own time, given the right conditions. He works with a broad range of clients and carries out a significant portion of his practice online.

Introduction

We stand on the brink of both unprecedented crisis and extraordinary possibility. The environmental systems that sustain us are edging towards a point of collapse, and yet our modern era also offers us unparalleled opportunities to reimagine our world and alleviate suffering. Yet instead of confronting these frightening and astonishing potentials, our society seems to be increasingly plagued by divisions that put us at war with each other, rather than uniting us to face the future together. Beneath this baffling avoidance lies the very same psychological processes that underpin many of the problems that we face in our personal lives, such as anger, addiction, depression, anxiety, and relationship issues. In order to find our way through these struggles, we must turn towards what we both fear and need the most: our dependency on each other.

At the centre of our difficulties lies a paradox: our connection to each other is both the cause and remedy for our wounds. Where we have been hurt in the past, we protect ourselves by closing off our connection to others, denying our need for their care and attempting instead to look after ourselves. Whilst this illusion of self-sufficiency helps us to survive, it comes at a great cost. When we cut ourselves off from our pain, we split ourselves psychologically, exiling the most vulnerable parts of ourselves that are in greatest need. We, like the society we live in, seek comfort in stories that sell us the idea that we are independent at the expense of dividing us from one another and our own deeper nature.

Stories are the lenses through which we see the world. They are the fundamental building blocks of psychological life, colouring our perception of everything and influencing us in ways that we are not even aware of. We need narratives to make sense of the world. They help us find meaning, order, identity, and safety. However, stories can be a double-edged sword, partnering with our own fear and pain to weave webs of denial that disconnect us from each other and exacerbate the divisions of sexism, racism, and bigotry of all kinds. This book follows the stories that we tell about ourselves and our need for others. It tracks them from their role in our early psychological development, through to their entanglements in our culture and finally into the therapy room itself. Like psychotherapy itself, this book is a journey to unearth the myths that we have taken as truths, so that we can uncover the hidden possibilities that lie beyond.

In changing our relationship to our need for others and allowing ourselves to be vulnerable, we can deal with the difficulties that we face in our relationships and emotional lives at their very core. This, of course, is not a straightforward journey. We need to face the shame that we have become caught up in and the blame that we direct at others. We must let our symptoms and difficulties take us into our darkest depths to confront the wounds and pain that we had hoped to leave behind. This journey into the underworld is an ancient tale, one that has taken numerous forms throughout history and been told in many different cultures around the globe. It is the myth of travelling to the most hellish places in order to recover something of incredible importance that has been lost. This book follows in the footsteps of this story, describing the voyage taken in the process of psychotherapy to reclaim the wounded parts of ourselves that we have banished with our denial. In making this journey, we may not only find healing for our own problems, but also come to tend the wounds that lie within the tangled roots of our interconnection and, in doing so, find a sense of existential security and support that no narrative can give us.

We begin by exploring how our psychological worlds are shaped during early childhood through the lens of developmental psychotherapy. In doing so, we discover how we build our maps of the world upon stories that make our experience of the world seem meaningful, consistent, and safe, but require us to deny elements of our experience. We follow this developmental arc further and examine how, when we grow up, we inevitably have experiences where our needs are not met. We deal with these by splitting off from the parts of ourselves that experience our unmet needs, leaving behind a vital piece of our being. The many different consequences that this has on our interpersonal relationships are explored in detail with stories from the therapy room alongside reflections on how these same difficulties present in the problems that we face as a society. We then study how the denial of our dependency splits our inner world in two and disconnects us from a greater interdependent wholeness, drawing on Buddhist ideas and the theories of Carl Jung. Returning to the therapy room, we follow the path to recovering our abandoned dependency and healing our wounded relationships through the process of psychotherapy. Lastly, we discover how in embracing our dependency, our interconnected nature is revealed, and we explore the profound implications this has for our personal lives and society at large.

A final word before we start our journey. It is worth keeping in mind that all narratives are incomplete truths. When we look at the world from a particular vantage point, our perspective both reveals and conceals aspects of a bigger picture. As we bring things into sharper focus, we lose sight of the background. Therefore, where the reflections in this book become increasingly specific, such as those on British culture and the problems in society, the more incomplete these views will inevitably become, and the greater there is potential for difference and division: this is inescapable. However, the intention of this book is not to promote a specific way of seeing the world, but rather to champion the value of reflection, so that we can hold our perspectives just a little less tightly and, in doing so, open up to experiencing the vastness of what lies beyond the stories we tell.

Client confidentiality

Confidentiality is the cornerstone of ethical psychotherapy practice. Confidentiality not only includes concealing a client's identity, but extends to handling and treating their stories with the same sensitive care that is embodied within the therapy itself. As psychotherapists, we all carry our clients' stories within us, and it is the spirit in which we hold them that reflects the care that is present in our work. For this reason, all case studies and dialogues used have been altered and amalgamated with other clinical material and experiences to create new narratives that any one client would not recognise as their own. The stories told, however, are essentially true in that they reflect many different aspects of real experiences and clinical practice.

CHAPTER 1

The storms of early dependency

Where did it all go wrong? Our messy lives and troubled world. Once upon a time, all was well and everything was in harmony. The birds sang hopefully at dawn, and the scent of wildflowers filled the air with their beauty. The Garden of Eden: paradise. There are many stories that speak of bygone golden eras. As a psychotherapist, I often hear my clients describe their childhoods as idyllic and trouble-free. It is easy to look at the distant past through rose-tinted glasses, looking for the hope and reassurance of knowing that somewhere, in a safe little bubble protected from harm, things are okay. However, in order to understand our relationship with dependency and vulnerability, we must travel back to our very earliest moments and dare to challenge the myths which keep the past innocent and uncontaminated.

It is hard to be a baby

Developmental psychotherapists are keen to remind us that the idea of early life being a time of quiet bliss is a fiction that conceals a very different reality. The infant's world is, in fact, a landscape of powerful psychological forces, some of which must be suffered through and endured. A baby is at the mercy of the world. It is totally vulnerable:

unable to feed, protect, or look after itself. It is entirely dependent on others for its survival and, as yet, is unable to even comprehend this. This is a time in a baby's development before they have established a sense of self: a feeling of "me" and "you". Like a second skin, this "self" will help protect and shelter the infant's inner world from the elements of the outer world. However, with this sense of separation comes the awareness of dependency: that this "I" relies on this "you" for survival. On top of this, the infant will soon realise that this "you" is entirely beyond their control. A disturbing and vulnerable position indeed.

But for now, let us return to the period of infancy before the perception of separateness arrives to complicate things: to the very early stages of development where the child's inner and outer worlds are one. This is a time before the infant has developed the skin of the self, leaving them entirely exposed to the world of outer events. Without this distinction, of inner and outer, there is no subject and object experience. The baby's experiential world is more like a changing landscape of scenery and weather. When things are well, it might look like a peaceful scene: a calm turquoise sea with the sun shining down on it. However, change is ever-present. For a baby, feelings like tiredness and hunger may emerge like clouds gathering over a previously peaceful ocean. Likewise, the outer world is also experienced as an aspect of the weather; for example, the smiling face of a parent brightens the sky with its warmth. The baby's carer senses their changing needs and moods, sheltering and providing for them accordingly. Seeing clouds gather, the infant's hunger is anticipated and satiated. The clouds dissipate, and the clear skies and tranquil ocean scene return … for now. For the infant, there is only now because at this stage of development, there is no perception of time. When the seas are calm and the sun is shining, there is eternal bliss.

It is not always possible to keep a baby happy, of course, and sooner or later paradise *is* lost. There will be many occasions where the clouds cannot be dissipated. Hunger, wind, tiredness and other discomforts grow, upsetting the equilibrium of the baby's world. Daniel Stern, a developmental psychotherapist, describes one such experience from the perspective of a baby:

> It is four hours since Joey's last feeding, and he is probably hungry. Suddenly, his lower lip protrudes. He starts to fret. Soon, the fretting gives way to jerky crying, then moves into a full cry.

> A storm threatens. The light turns metallic. The march of clouds across the sky breaks apart. Pieces of sky fly off in different directions. The wind picks up force in silence. There are rushing sounds, but no motion. The wind and its sound have separated. Each chases after its lost partner in fits and starts. The world is disintegrating. Something is about to happen.
>
> Uneasiness grows. It spreads from the center and turns into pain.
>
> It is at the center that the storm breaks out. It is at the very center that it grows stronger and turns into pulsing waves. These waves push the pain out, then pull it back again.
>
> The wind and the sound and the pieces of the sky are all pulled back into the center. There they find one another again, are reunited. Only to be thrown outward and away, then sucked back to form the next wave-darker and stronger.
>
> The pulsing waves swell to dominate the whole weatherscape. The world is howling. Everything explodes and is blown out and then collapses and rushes back toward a knot of agony that cannot last—but does.[1]

These violent "weatherscapes" can seem devastating and eternal to the infant, whose sense of time has not yet developed. It is not just hunger that haunts a baby's world. Other crises conjure up their own unique landscapes of suffering. To drown or be flooded with overwhelming stimuli. To be parched and dry like a desert. Or to feel the uncontrolled overflowing expansion of space as the baby is let go of instead of being tightly held. Sometimes the baby's world is more like the scene of an apocalypse than the Garden of Eden.

Memories hidden before our eyes

As time goes on and the infant develops and grows, both the experiences of tranquillity and catastrophe recede into the background. Alongside developing a sense of self and others, infants learn an appreciation of events and time. The everlasting quality of the present moment takes on a different feel as the child's developing mental apparatus begins to make the world feel increasingly more manageable. Fast forward to the present day, where we exist in an extremely complex web of mental conceptions that produce our experience of a sense of self that endures through time and an outer world that we feel as though we understand.

It requires a great stretch of the imagination to even contemplate what life might have been like before these mental formulations had developed. Yet in the recesses of our minds, outside of conscious awareness, the memory and impact of our timeless experiences of both apocalypse and bliss live on.

One of the fundamental premises of developmental psychotherapy is that the experiences of our past shape the way in which we see the present. What we live through lays down the foundations for how we come to see and make sense of the world. We form maps, templates and stories that help us navigate through life. The very earliest experiences we have as babies and infants inform the outlines of our most fundamental assumptions about life. For example, at some point in time we would have learnt that day follows night. This seems so obvious that it is hard to imagine that on at least one occasion, the light of the morning would have come as an incredible and unexpected revelation. Over time, as we learn, we stop needing to consult our maps consciously; we do it automatically. The maps of our world soon come to be experienced as our reality. They become unquestionably real, and we become totally unaware that we are seeing the world through the lens of a map or story. Of course, experiences that happen as we grow older will continue to mould and shape our perceptions of the world. But what makes these very early experiences unique is that they are so foundational that it is almost impossible to be aware of them. They become like a pair of glasses that we view everything through. They are so close to our eyes that we cannot see the lenses and even forget that we are wearing spectacles in the first place. Early experiences, therefore, inform the very essence of how we perceive both ourselves and the world, all the while we remain totally unaware of their presence.

Perhaps the most important template we will create is our sense of self. Every experience we have growing up contributes to a growing perception of "who" and "what" we are. The very earliest experiences inform the most fundamental aspects, the bones, of the story we have about our self. As the experience of forming the self and discovering an "other" occurs during the time when we, as infants, rely entirely on our caregivers, the meaning we construct about dependency is woven into the most basic and fundamental maps of who we are. What it means to rely on another person, to be dependent, relates to the very core components and meanings that our sense of self is built on. When you pull on the thread of dependency, the whole fabric of our sense of self can feel under threat.

Our early experiences, of both idyllic blissful oneness and terrifying Earth-shattering storms, lie just beneath the surface outside of our awareness, but nevertheless, powerfully determine how we perceive the world. They are some of the first threads with which we weave the tapestries of the stories that come to define our sense of self. They silently wield their power, controlling us without our knowledge. They emerge in our imaginations and stories as visions of heaven and hell and mingle with our deepest hopes and fears for the future. But it is love, most of all, that has the power to awaken these hidden memories from their slumber.

Cupid's arrow

Relationship difficulties are one of the most common reasons that lead people to seek out psychotherapy, and one of the most frequent ways in which people encounter a lack of control over their own emotions and behaviours. As adults, perhaps the most significant way in which our hidden memories of dependency exercise their control over us is in the sphere of our closest and most intimate relationships.

To be struck by Cupid's arrow is to be carried away by a power beyond conscious awareness: to lose control of our own destiny and to be propelled by a force beyond our understanding. Love can inspire actions that seem crazy, such as starting the Trojan War for Helen of Troy, or standing outside your teen crush's house with a boombox in the rain, singing along to their favourite song. Equally, jealous rages and "crimes of passion" are dramatic losses of control that happen under a love spell. Whilst love and being in love cannot be reduced to these psychological forces alone, the experience of love undoubtedly re-evokes the hopes and fears of our very earliest experiences. Cupid, it was said, followed his mother Venus' orders and would wound whomever she chose with his arrow. Behind the scenes of the wild and crazy behaviour that falling in love can bring out of us, Venus and Cupid, a mother and baby, are at work. The drive for total merger with another person, to find union, has echoes of our earliest memories of blissful oneness, where serenity is all-enveloping. To fall in love is to allow ourselves to be carried away by the fantasy that this other person is all we need (and can meet all our needs). This state can have a timeless feel, which is reminiscent of the eternal experiences we had before our capacity to conceive of time had developed. However, this bubble of timeless perfection can unexpectedly burst when we are let down in even the smallest ways. This does not just give rise to regular disappointment, but can conjure back up the ferocity of the storms that we experienced when our needs were not met in the state of deep dependency as babies.

Whilst love is where our loss of agency can feel most exaggerated, all kinds of intimacy can make us feel as though we are losing control. But what is it about being close to someone else that brings these long-forgotten memories to life? To be intimate with somebody is to let ourselves want and need someone else without the usual cautions that keep us protected. It is to allow the fulfilment of our hopes to rest entirely in the hands of another. This is the experience of being vulnerable.

Vulnerability

Vulnerability is our ancient companion. It is a relationship that stretches back to the distant past, predating even our human ancestors. Being aware of danger is fundamental to all animals, whose brains are hard-wired to detect and respond to threat at a fundamentally instinctual level. Part of our being human is our ability to consciously evaluate, think, and consider situations and to evaluate a hazard using our conscious minds. However, it is important to understand that, like other animals, a lot of our reactions and responses to threat also occur at a preconscious instinctual level. Because of this, we may not always be aware of the ways in which we protect ourselves.

What makes humans especially unique is the extent to which we have evolved to depend entirely on others for survival. It is easy to understand how this is the case for a newborn baby, but it also holds true that adult humans have depended on their communities for survival throughout history. Being isolated or exiled from your tribe would have meant imminent death for many of our distant ancestors, who would have depended on their community for survival. This is one of the reasons why our social relationships and place within our society feel like life and death matters, and why we have evolved to dedicate so much of our intelligence towards attuning to others and understanding relationships. Being vulnerable can therefore include something that puts your relationship with another, or the tribe, in question. Consequently, our relationships with each other and our communities are largely governed by our subconscious minds, which, unbeknownst to us, influence our behaviour to protect our vulnerability.

However, vulnerability is not something that can be avoided. It is necessary to expose yourself to degrees of risk in almost every endeavour. In our hunter-gatherer past, this would have meant putting ourselves in peril every time we went hunting, but the same is true today when we drive to work and risk a potential car accident. Whilst our physical dangers are much less considerable in our modern world, there are elements of vulnerability in almost everything we do. For example, in approaching a stranger, we might make a life-long friend or even meet a lover. However, it is also possible we will have an argument or experience some kind of social rejection or humiliation. There is no escaping the unknowable nature of the future, which can dish out good and bad fortune in equal measure. However, you can be certain that in order to do anything in life, you must take some risk. Shaking hands is said to have its origins in showing somebody that you are not carrying a weapon. It is necessary to be vulnerable, to take a chance and put down your defences to open yourself up to the possibilities that life presents.

The hope of finding what we seek is what makes taking a risk worthwhile. Where there is hope, there is both possibility and vulnerability. To connect with someone, we need to venture outside of ourselves: to allow our fate to rest in the hands of another. When we allow ourselves to hope, we are exposing ourselves to the possibility of being deeply let down and hurt. We are depending on another. In every possibility for connection, hope lives alongside the vulnerability of dependency.[2]

Subconscious protection

In this constant dance between hope and fear, hope does not always prevail. Sometimes it does not feel safe to be vulnerable. Our vulnerability has real consequences, physically, emotionally, and psychologically.

Based on our evaluations of the risk, where we consult our past experiences, we may decide to err on the side of caution. This can be a process that happens totally outside of our conscious awareness, leaving our own behaviour to become a mystery to us. For example, inexplicable uprisings of anger are often a strong indication that there is a vulnerability present that we are defending, but are not fully aware of. When our conscious attitudes are different to our behaviour, it is usually a sign that we have some kind of defensive response occurring outside of our conscious awareness.

Nowhere is the mismatch between our intentions and our actions more pronounced than in our intimate relationships. In its promise and threat to touch us deeply, closeness evokes our deepest hopes and fears, and we may often find ourselves at the mercy of both our subconscious longings and defences. In intimate relationships, this can lead to a state of inner conflict and ambivalence, where the hope to connect clashes with the drive to keep us safe. At any given moment, either of these impulses may be directing our actions, irrespective of whether they are within or outside of our conscious awareness. When our actions are driven by our subconscious mind, but our conscious awareness has other ideas, it can create a state of feeling incredibly torn and confused when it comes to romantic relationships. For example, we may really want to find a life partner, yet find ourselves breaking off all our relationships just as they start to blossom. This is often labelled a "commitment issue", even though it is often the vulnerability that commitment exposes that is feared, rather than commitment itself. Consciously, we are trying to get close to someone, but our unconscious mind is making the decision to protect us from the risk that comes with the vulnerability of emotional intimacy. It is equally possible to have an experience of consciously wanting to separate from someone, but being compelled by subconscious forces to stay. Often, this clash between how we want to behave and how we are behaving will be what brings somebody to therapy, along with the hope that they can bring their inexplicable behaviour back in line with their conscious agenda. However, the solution to this psychic conflict is rarely to side with the client in their war against their subconscious mind. Rather, we need to provide the right support for the client, so that they are able to feel safe enough to face their vulnerability and therefore, to be able to experience both their hopes and fears consciously. This is a process we will cover in much more detail later on; however, for now, let us return to our growing baby and the journey of its development.

Towards independence

As we grow older, we become progressively able to meet our own needs, moving from dependency towards becoming independent.[3] On the way, we find that for some of our needs, we need to rely on ourselves more than we had hoped. This is often a reflection of the care that is available around us. If we grow up in a house with eight siblings, we may well end up learning to dress ourselves sooner than an only child, as a parent with a spare pair of hands would probably be a rare occurrence. This is no bad thing and part of normal and healthy development. We soon learn to fill the gaps between what we need from others and what we get. These ever-widening gaps present us with new challenges; in responding to them, we grow. Care is both physical and emotional, so many of these needs and subsequent gaps will be psychological or emotional in nature. For example, as babies we need to be soothed when we cry, but over time, we learn to internalise the care we are given, and in moments when we are not being soothed by our caregiver we self-soothe.

Some gaps, however, are too big. This could involve the actual neglect of a fundamental need, or, more commonly, a subtle psychological or emotional need that goes unrecognised and therefore gets persistently overlooked. When there is such a gap, the shortfall of care given is too big to bridge on our own. We are forced to meet our own needs in a situation where it is not yet possible to properly do so. Instead of becoming a stimulus to growth, this becomes a source of trauma. We are stretched beyond what we are capable of, leaving us out of shape and having to cope in a self-sufficient way that does not properly fulfil us. In order to manage, we resort to denial, banishing our unmet need out of mind and out of sight, a process we will explore in more detail in Chapter 3.

Yet, someday, we may find ourselves in a relationship where, on a deeper level, it starts to feel possible that this unmet need could finally be fulfilled. This hope, however, also triggers the fear of the vulnerability that comes with wanting something from another that we have no control over. Our early subconscious memories of dependency are activated, facing us with the possibility of both blissful satiation and apocalyptic let-down. Torn between protecting our vulnerability and the promise of finding deep fulfilment, we begin the tumultuous journey of reuniting with our denied need for others.

Sarah

One of the places where our denied needs are reawakened from their hibernation is in therapy. The non-judgemental, warm and attuned presence of an interested therapist can provide a greenhouse-like environment to the dormant seeds of unmet needs. Sensing that perhaps something is possible here and now, that was not possible before, the seeds of hope germinate. However, as hope resurfaces, so too do the memories of how these needs went unmet in the first place and the self-protective cautions that were developed in order to keep those needs hidden and safe.

Let us look at how this all comes together in a snapshot of psychotherapy with Sarah, an English literature professor, who came to therapy suffering from depression and loneliness. Sarah was very charming and likeable. When she arrived for a session, she would always ask me how I was, make a joke or two and then a silence would follow before she began talking about herself. Over time, I became aware of just how interesting and engaging her stories were, but often wondered how much she was having to compromise her emotional reality in order to make her anecdotes so entertaining.

As therapy progressed, the usual silence at the beginning of the session became longer. During the sessions, she would recount her week in a very lively way before falling into a long silence. These silences seemed to fill with increasing distress for her. Her brow would furrow, and she would fix her gaze on the floor. I felt a powerful atmosphere of confusion fill the room like a fog. Despite finding it hard to have a clear thought in these moments, I felt my senses heighten and would often feel a strong knotted sensation in the pit of my stomach. Whilst uncomfortable, the silences felt incredibly intimate. Even when she was not looking at me, it seemed as if she were acutely aware of my presence. It felt as though I was waiting for Sarah to emerge like a scared animal being tempted out of hiding with food, as if caught between the intense longing to open up, but also frozen with fear at the prospect of exposing her vulnerability, without her "entertaining stories" for protection.

Over time, the contrast between these periods of silence and her anecdotes mellowed. She began to share her emotions with me more openly and would increasingly talk about what it was like for her growing up. She described how her parents were so preoccupied that she was left feeling as though she was not sure if they were interested in her at all. "It must be because I'm not really that special," she told herself. Underneath her words lay the unbearable pain of feeling unwanted and unlovable.

In her relationships and within therapy, Sarah became aware of how she had learnt to take care of everyone else's needs. In shaping herself around the other person by being attentive, understanding, and good company, she was actually protecting herself from the risky situation of exposing what she felt was her unlovable self. This was how she had learnt to cope with feeling as though others were not interested in her: her self-sufficient armour. Whilst, on the one hand, she desperately longed for deeper relationships, she was subconsciously keeping people at a distance in order to protect herself from re-experiencing the pain of feeling unwanted that would be triggered should she feel as though someone was not interested in her. Sarah's furrowed brow is her body's way of expressing the tension of holding back the terrifying psychic conflict that is raging just below her conscious awareness, and the knotted sensation that I felt was my body's way of hearing her experience. The fog of confusion that filled the therapy room signalled the presence of the denial and shame that are attempting to keep this conflict safely submerged beneath conscious awareness.

For Sarah, therapy was a place where her unmet need for being related to with genuine interest could re-emerge. Whilst on the surface her therapy was just an opportunity to be really listened to, it reawakened all the power and intensity that belongs to the very earliest stages of life: to have her life essence reflected back at her through the shining eyes of an interested parent. Because of this, it also evoked the terrors of early developmental disappointments: finding a dead and lonely landscape behind absent eyes. Through therapy, Sarah was able to feel safe and hopeful enough to brave re-exposing her authentic self to the world and was rewarded with the newfound sense of authenticity and aliveness that came with connecting more deeply with herself and others.

Summary

Our time as babies is spent in a state of total dependency that can be both blissful and terrifying. As we grow up, we build maps and templates of the world that we subconsciously use to understand ourselves and the world as adults. Our need for others triggers the hopes and fears of our intense early experiences of dependency and influences us in ways that can be baffling to us, particularly in our closest and most intimate relationships. Where our psychological needs have not been met adequately by others, we make do with self-sufficient adaptations and bury our need for others. Despite this, our subconscious desire and fear of opening up remains and can re-emerge where there is hope that our needs may finally be met. We face our vulnerability and dependency on a daily basis, but rather than confront its terrifying power, we learn to suppress the powerful feelings and predicaments that it evokes. Denial, the subject of the next chapter, comes to define our relationship to dependency.

CHAPTER 2

The stories of denial

> *Only a great story can shelter us.*
> —John Moriarty[4]

Denial has a hidden hand in weaving the stories that come to define our realities. These narratives attempt to give us a feeling of stability, safety, and control, but can end up causing more insecurity than they solve. The outlook of British culture on dependency is a case in point. On the surface, British culture extolls the virtues of independence, strength, and control; however, beneath these sentiments lie skeletons in the closet that haunt our collective psyche. By exploring the stories we cling to for safety, we can begin to understand the full cost that denial demands of us.

Denial: The silent assassin

Denial is, at its core, a potent and mysterious psychological process. When we merely ignore something, we do so with choice and conscious awareness. Denial, however, is different: it is a process that happens completely outside of our awareness. It is like a silent assassin that works under the cover of darkness. Not only is the target of denial taken out, but no witnesses to the murder can be allowed to survive either, with the assassin falling on their own blade to complete the mission.

Whilst it has a dark side, denial is an essential companion to our day-to-day functioning. It is a necessary evil. As we go about our days, we are constantly relying on and following the maps that we have drawn up for ourselves in the past. This is a process that all happens beneath our conscious awareness, and denial is essential to it running smoothly. Whilst our subconscious mind is busy navigating the world using the templates we have previously constructed, our conscious mind, our awareness, can focus on what is new. If this were not the case, we would constantly be bewildered each moment of the day, still stuck perhaps at marvelling at the sensations of what our fingers feel like or confused as to why the world disappears when we close our eyelids. Whilst these were once conscious concerns, we soon enough make up our minds about their meaning and commit these interpretations to our bank of subconscious templates. Anything that we subsequently encounter that contradicts these maps, but seems insignificant enough not to address consciously, is denied. This process can be observed in our opinions: most of us make up our minds about an issue and then put it to bed. It is only when presented with a substantial argument to the contrary that we may consider reviewing the facts of the matter once again and consciously facing the dilemma that they present us with. We have our stories and, on the whole, we stick to them. In moderation, this lets us get on with our lives without overwhelming our limited conscious awareness or enduring the upheaval that comes with changing our minds every day. This helps to foster a sense of psychological stability and consistency: qualities we hope to find in our sense of self and in the world around us. In reality, neither ourselves nor the world is as understandable, consistent, and predictable as we would wish they were, and we often have to deny many different aspects of our experience in order to maintain these illusions of security.

The Emperor's new clothes

Perhaps the most defining aspect of our humanness is the fact that we are storytellers. The stories we tell each other in order to make sense of the world make up the tapestries of our cultures and provide us with psychological shelter from having to understand our experience all on our own. These subconscious stories, that we create for ourselves and absorb from our culture, are like a pair of shoes that we put on without thinking each day to protect us from the harsh sensations of walking barefoot on the ground. They insulate us from the unknowable nature of reality and let us get on with life without coming up against an overwhelming existential encounter every step of the way. So, we go about our lives dressed in the stories that keep us safe and warm, with our narratives woven together to form the clothing of our sense of self, identity, and worldview. However, this means that when our culture, beliefs, or values are brought into question, it can feel as though the very fabric of our being is under attack.

At times, we may find that our own experience does not match up with the stories that are being told around us. Whether that is being gay in a homophobic society, an atheist in a religious town, or having right-wing political views in a left-wing family. This is a difficult place to be. It does not feel safe to see the world in a drastically different way from the rest of our tribe. However, it can feel equally dangerous and unnerving to be in possession of a map that does not bear resemblance to the landscape we are surveying before us. This presents a very difficult dilemma: we can either choose the safety of fitting into our collective, at the expense of distancing ourselves from our own experience, or we can opt for the security of having a map that fits the terrain better, but face the threat of social isolation. Where we do choose to fit in, we have to deal with the problem that our own sensory experience does not fully match the narratives of the culture that we are adopting. To have the self-perception that our map of the world is compromised would feel extremely destabilising. To deal with this predicament, denial steps in, hiding the perception of our senses from us, and giving us the illusion of safety that we get from feeling as if we understand the world. We tell ourselves that we think we do what we do because of the reasons and justifications that we give ourselves, rather than being aware of the subconscious processes and motivations that are really in charge of the show. This "rationalisation" works hand-in-hand with denial to make sure our narratives feel sufficiently strong and real to meet our need for psychological stability.

The stories we tell, however, are subjective and imperfect maps. Therefore, if they are to provide the sense of safety and stability that is essential to their function, it is necessary that we hide their flawed nature from ourselves. It simply will not do to "believe" in them; we must feel as if they *are* the truth. Any witness that is aware of their tenuous and fragile nature must be killed. This is a dangerous combination: to be in possession of such an inherent vulnerability and to be compelled, without conscious choice, to defend it as if our life depended upon it.

What are you wearing?

It is a strange exercise to question our own most fundamental viewpoints, as the most central feature of our relationship to them is that we are in denial about the fact that they are merely a "belief" in the first place. Is our modern paradigm an exception to this, given that the scientific method has finally given us an objective map of reality? Perhaps, however, to take this view means that for the entirety of human history, everyone else has been fundamentally mistaken, even though they undoubtedly would have felt the same sense of certainty and had an equally impassioned justification for why they "know" and do not merely "believe". The more firmly we stand behind our own perspective, the further we stand apart from the rest of humanity.

It is easy to see the absurdity of denial in others, but almost impossible to be aware of it in ourselves. Take climate change denial as an example. From my perspective, it takes quite a lot of mental gymnastics to deny the vast amounts of scientific evidence that points to climate change occurring as a result of human activity. Changing your mind, or someone else's, about such a major issue is no small feat. This is because altering a single piece of the jigsaw within the internal model we have constructed, drawn from various narratives and maps that we have incorporated, can threaten the cohesion of the entire structure. Different political beliefs, social identities, ideologies, and values all form a complex web of interconnecting components that need to mesh together as coherently as possible if we are to feel secure in our identities and perceptions of the world. Any ill-fitting pieces of the puzzle are major threats to the stability of our paradigm and will cause "cognitive dissonance": the discomfort of holding ideas in close proximity in our minds that do not fit together. In order to manage the ways in which our stories of the world do not fully make sense or present us with other problematic challenges, we avoid looking at the questionable seams and hide our awareness of them from ourselves totally. We deny them. Therefore, to ask somebody who does not believe in climate change to change their mind may necessitate a total reconfiguring of the way they look at life and their place in society. Consequently, when you present somebody with a puzzle piece that does not fit their picture, it is understandable that they reject it with vigour. It is akin to offering someone the opportunity to either have a mental breakdown or face social ostracisation.

It is easier to cast judgement on others than it is to try to understand their outlook. However, if I really try, I can imagine what my viewpoint might look like from the perspective of someone who does not believe in climate change. In fact, they probably see my belief in climate change as part of an elaborate denial of the truth that I am under the spell of. Perhaps from their perspective, I am protecting myself from the terrifying reality that the media are being controlled by political forces that are covertly pushing their agenda and hiding the truth about what is going on in order to control the general public. Ironically, this is a near mirror image of how I might view their psychological constructions. Perhaps we are not so different after all.

At this point, I invite you to stop reading for a moment and take note of your own thought processes and feelings as you finish reading this section. Talking about our most precious core beliefs, with the suggestion that they are merely subjective, is threatening. Perhaps you are able to observe some tension in your body. It may be that you notice some thoughts that seek to justify your belief system or attack the suggestion that these beliefs might be subjective. Defending and shoring up our own narratives is a universal and natural process, no matter how we see the world.

Identity war

We all have stories that we use to make sense of the world that are intrinsically linked to our own identities. These are the very stories that form our sense of self and make us feel real in this world. Naturally, we protect the stories that are most precious to us, that we feel *are* us. Other narratives that challenge our own can therefore feel as though they threaten us at a deep existential level just by virtue of existing. The potential of war lies here, like a coiled spring ready to unleash its polarising energy at the slightest provocation. It is easy to trigger a process where the justification of our own narrative demands an increasing denial of the others'. This justification is often experienced as an attack by the other party, which triggers a corresponding defensive response. As each perspective is challenged, each will need to increasingly justify and defend themselves. Soon, each other's very presence is experienced as an existential threat to reality itself. The sudden energy release of this expanding spring can explode as bombs are exchanged in the wars between cultures and nations, or erupt as a domestic argument that appears out of nowhere on a Sunday afternoon.

In order to psychologically invest, to believe in a narrative, it is necessary to deny the other stories that are in conflict with its vision. The more fervently that we cling to the literal and concrete nature of a story, the darker the shadow of denial we will cast and the more alienated we become from each other. When we cast our stories in iron and use them as shields against each other, rather than as temporary shelter from the elements, we find ourselves stuck inside cages that we originally built to protect us. The more we try to hold onto the existential security that our narratives promise, the more solid our stories become and the deeper we perceive our division, which itself brings a feeling of existential threat. The only way out of this downward spiral is to brave the vulnerability of loosening our grip on our stories and opening up to the unknowable nature of the world.

A monopoly on truth

It is difficult to talk about denial without suggesting that we have ownership of the truth. If every way of looking at the world is subjective, denial is a judgement that can never be made with any certainty. This presents some very challenging and important dilemmas for psychotherapists such as myself.

Are there untrue, immoral, or pathological ways of looking at the world? Should we try to influence the way our clients see the world? At one end of the spectrum, challenging bigoted views can easily be seen as an ethical obligation, but at what point does pushing against someone's beliefs become an enforcement of our own ideologies and an abuse of power? Holding the view that a client is in denial is, in one sense, to dismiss a client's authority over their own experience. We must interpret denial in our clients only with utmost care, recognising the profound impact it is likely to have on their sense of psychological stability, given the gravity they are likely to give to the authority of our interpretations. Even if we take the position that we should not attempt to change our clients' views, our own opinions, beliefs, and perspectives inevitably bleed into our responses, whether we like it or not. Influencing our clients from a position of power is almost certainly unavoidable.

When we notice that we are holding the view that our client is in denial, it is important to reflect on the origins of this opinion. Does it stem from witnessing an inconsistency in what the client is saying that suggests that they themselves actually hold other conflicting views subconsciously? Or does it stem from a difference in how we see the world? When we feel that our own narratives are under threat, we may feel compelled to defend and bolster our own position, rather than prioritise the process of therapy. It is difficult to be consciously aware of this process, as when our stories are threatened we are usually in the grip of our own denial. However, we may get a clue as to when this process is occurring if we pay attention to the sensations and feelings in our body. Whilst our minds may be under the spell of denial when our narratives are challenged, our bodies are likely to register the threat. This can sometimes be felt as a bodily change or sensation; by being mindful of it, we can facilitate a deeper awareness and understanding of what is happening between ourselves and our client. This may help us to mitigate the need to "act out" a defensive response. Having reflected on whether we are in the grip of our own defensive agenda, how best should we approach "denial" in our clients? First, it is important to keep in mind that in acknowledging denial, the fact that the stories we are telling ourselves are imperfect, puts us in an incredibly vulnerable position. Any attempt to push on this tender spot will naturally be met by a defensive response that will shut down the vulnerable process of opening up. With this in mind, we need to give our clients acceptance, space, and understanding, so that we can create a safe enough environment for them to uncover and connect with the vulnerability that lies beneath these protective stories. When a client feels like they no longer need to protect themselves, they are able to unravel the web of conflicting and intersecting stories that make up their identity and worldview and find new ways of seeing things that are more open and inclusive to their experience, requiring less denial.

Justifying injustice

It is not only our own personal psychologies that are made up of interconnecting stories; our cultures are also a patchwork of interwoven narratives that attempt to present themselves as infallible perspectives. Looking at British culture with an appreciation that it is, in part, a story that attempts to create stability, security, and comfort, what can we see of the shadow it casts? What has it been necessary to deny in order to achieve coherence in this story? As acknowledged earlier, there is a dilemma in interpreting denial. In telling my own story about our culture, it will undoubtedly reflect the biases in my own perspective as much as it will shed light on the blind spots that I am addressing. Nevertheless, it is necessary to cast a shadow if we are to stand anywhere with solidity.

British culture tells us all to stand on our own two feet. Independence is praised, individual freedom held in the highest regard, power and autonomy fetishised, and dependency feared. The front pages of our newspapers publicise this obsession almost daily, with headlines appearing about asylum seekers and benefit "cheats". The very idea that somebody might be being supported more than they can give back constitutes a national scandal. Whilst caring for someone else might be admired, to be cared for by another is a taboo that haunts our national psyche. Why is independence so important to us? Or perhaps it is more telling to ask: what does feeling independent shield us from as a culture?

Placing independence at the forefront of Britain's national identity conceals the very opposite truth: that Britain is actually especially dependent on the rest of the world. This reliance is kept hidden, as acknowledging it would expose the dark underbelly of Britain's colonial roots and the exploitation of people and resources that this necessitates. Colonialism attempts to create a safe, protected bubble for those inside it, keeping the atrocities needed to maintain this illusion of safety out of sight and out of mind. Britain continues today with this "island mentality", safe in the knowledge that war and poverty are "out there" and not "in here" (despite over one in five Britons living in poverty[5]). Britain *has* to think of itself as an independent, disconnected island, or it would be forced to reckon with the dark shadow of its relationships.

The ghost of our colonial history still lingers in the recesses of our cultural psyche. It is not fully denied, but neither is it brought into the light. In a very British way, it is "fudged" and our colonial culture lives on. Just as it is impossible to apologise whilst you are still committing a crime, it is difficult to admit guilt whilst still pocketing from the spoils of inequality. Britain is, of course, not one homogenised population and privileged groups within society benefit more from these power structures and the denial of both their existence and impact. The more that you benefit from a particular way of looking at things, the harder it is to see things in any other way. For those with marginalised identities and histories of oppression, the shadow of Britain's colonialism will be much easier to see.[6] Denial, which manicures our stories so that they are acceptable to us, makes it difficult to see both present inequalities and aspects of history that challenge a British identity which sees itself as being fair, just and "civilised". When these injustices do come to public consciousness, explanatory narratives are needed to justify the behaviour of our society. In order to treat others badly, it is necessary to see them as being less worthy of care. When you find yourself behaving in a way that you are not proud of, you have two options: you can either face the difficulty of incorporating something into your identity that you prefer was not there, or you can explain to yourself why your behaviour makes sense and is the right thing to do. This is to justify injustice. It is the unconscious driver that, over time, leads us to see those who benefit less from the society we are part of as being less worthy of benefit.

Looking down upon dependency, vulnerability, and being in need is deeply woven into British culture and identity. When we are immersed in such a culture, we subconsciously internalise and enact these judgements towards ourselves, rejecting our own dependency and vulnerability with a "stiff upper lip". This leaves us ill-equipped as a culture to deal with the feeling of powerlessness that comes with needing others. It teaches us that needing others is a deficiency and that our dependency and vulnerability are enemies that are to be feared and avoided. It pits us against fundamental aspects of our emotional repertoire and necessitates that we cut ourselves off from huge swathes of both our inner and outer worlds. The extent of denial needed to maintain this position creates an inherent instability and fragility that will always be a fight to maintain.

An ecology of stories

Our history is the thread from which we weave the stories of our culture and identities. When we hide from our own history, the garment that is meant to keep us warm will have holes in it. When we only have the materials to craft a narrative that relies heavily on denial, other stories will feel threatening, and therefore our ability to be open to understanding the perspectives of others will be fundamentally compromised. In order to find a sense of deeper security in relationship to the stories we hold, we need to not only open up to our own history, but to the unknowable nature of the world that feels so threatening. The more that we learn to tolerate the feelings of uncertainty that arise when we genuinely open to understanding others who differ from us, the more existentially secure we will become. Furthermore, as we are increasingly able to truly let in and understand the worldview of others, we are enriched with a diversity of threads with which we can integrate into a more comprehensive narrative of our own. In the same way that diversity creates robustness and adaptability in our ecosystems, having a more profound understanding of a multitude of perspectives gives our sense of self and reality a flexible stability that allows us to open and connect to the world more deeply.

Summary

Stories are the way in which we understand and experience the world. When we adopt a narrative, it becomes a subconscious template, and we deny conflicting experiences and perspectives in order to maintain our sense of psychological stability and identity within a group. Denial is therefore subjective, which is important to consider carefully, especially in the context of psychotherapy. It is in our interest to question the meanings of the stories we tell ourselves and absorb from our cultures. In British culture, dependency is stigmatised and denied due to its colonial history. This contributes to the already difficult task of coping with our vulnerability and results in an insecure and defensive outlook on the world that alienates us from each other and the depths of our human experience.

CHAPTER 3

The denial of dependency

When the care that we need is unavailable, we resort to denial in order to cope, abandoning our need for others. In addition to being an assassin, denial is a storyteller, arranging the scene of the crime in a way that places the victim in the role of murderer. Instead of seeing the heartbreaking ways in which we have been let down, we end up blaming ourselves and carrying this hidden shame into our futures. Unfortunately, turning against our vulnerability in this way comes with tragic consequences for our relationships and society.

Life's lessons

As we grow up, we learn which behaviours are welcome in our relationships with others and which are not. For example, a child who is ignored when they cry, but is paid attention to when angry, may go on to learn that when they feel sad, they are better off shouting than bursting into tears. As highly sophisticated social and emotional creatures, we form intricate and complex understandings about relationships that become blueprints that persist in our subconscious minds. The lessons we learn about dependency and about our own needs are mostly formed early on in our development, but will fundamentally shape how we will relate to others for the rest of our lives.

One of the most elusive teachers of these lessons is the invisible web of culture that permeates our world with its narratives. We soak up its teachings slowly over time like a sponge. The ideals of our culture need not be written on billboards for us to see; we can sense them all around us in the tiniest of details that often fly under our conscious radars. Often it is not what is said, but how it is said, or even what is not said, that carries the greatest power. For example, it may be that our subconscious mind registers the tone of voice in which a sitcom character says the word "needy", which gives us the impression that to be "needy" is to be undesirable. Or perhaps it is the facial expression we see on another's face as they glance towards a homeless person who is asking for money. The meanings and associations that we learn can all occur without us having any conscious awareness that they are taking place. Nevertheless, over time, all these subtle signals paint a picture that we internalise unknowingly, shaping the relationship that we have with our own needs and with dependency itself.

Less subtly, it is the way in which we learn to relate to our own needs and dependency through the way in which we are directly treated by others. These are lessons that can hit home suddenly and with great impact. When our needs are rejected outright, the message that they are not wanted is hammered home with painful force: moments of really longing to be cared for and reaching out, only to be met with painful rejection. "Where's my brave boy gone?" a client's parents would ask whenever he cried. "Never again will I put myself in such a vulnerable position" we tell ourselves as we squash down and lock away our cries for care, inadvertently repeating this rejection inwardly.

Lastly, we can learn that our dependent needs are problematic through the repeated absence of their fulfilment. A child will stop crying if their parents never come to comfort them. They learn that their need for soothing will not be met by the world and are forced to make up the deficit in self-sufficient ways. Sometimes, however, what we need is overlooked in much more subtle ways. Perhaps the particular type of care that we require is not accurately recognised, or the environment of our upbringing makes it difficult to fulfil. It may be that our caregivers have their own psychological blocks that prevent them from really seeing or attending to us properly. An absence like this can leave us feeling that what we need and want, in our relationships with others, is either fundamentally not available or impossible to attain. Like the pair of glasses we forget we are wearing, this belief can become an unquestionable certainty. For example, for someone who has learnt that their own tears will never be soothed, it is easy to look at a crying child and not see the need for comfort, but rather see the necessity for a child to learn to control their own sobs.

Trauma fence

When we are left feeling as though our need for others is not welcome, we find ourselves in an impossible and painful situation. Not only do we not have something that we require, but we also have to deal with a painful sense of rejection. To make matters worse, we are left to tend to this wound all by ourselves. Often, however, this is beyond what we are psychologically capable of, as we first have to learn how to care for ourselves by being cared for by others. When we have not had this experience, we are left in a hopeless position: without what we need and unable to ask for help. Because of this, we are left totally unable to move forward psychologically, trapped in a frozen state of trauma.

Without someone there to care for us, all that is left at our disposal to cope is denial. In order to carry on, we are forced to psychologically ring-fence the whole problematic area, so that its pain and impossibility do not impede the rest of our psychological lives. To erect this boundary, we tell ourselves a story about why this has happened to us. This process is like hemming a piece of frayed material: meanings are woven around our wound in order to make sense of it and maintain the integrity of our psychological templates. A common theme in these stories is that we blame ourselves. Whilst this may seem counterintuitive, it often seems both more likely and more manageable to us than the alternative: of thinking that the powerful caregivers that we are totally dependent on are unable to look after us properly. By telling ourselves that it is our need that is the issue, we make the problem feel smaller and in some way under our own control. We find explanations as to why our needs must be unreasonable or unwarranted. Often, we need not look far to find the thread of a compatible story with which we can weave into our own.

Through the experiences we have as individuals and the messages we receive from our culture, we create meanings about our own needs and those of others. For example, we might learn "If I reach out, people will move away" or "People will become angry with me when I'm sad". These meanings also usually carry a subtext: the explanation that we tell ourselves to make sense of them. For example, "People move away from me when I reach out *because* needing other people is weak and repulsive" or "If I become sad, people will become angry with me *because* it is selfish and ugly to be sad". These impressions come to form how we see ourselves and the world. When we make a judgement about our own needs, we also apply it to the needs of others and recount the same stories that were told to us, feeding back into the cultural milieu. Perhaps we even find ourselves saying to our crying child: "Where's my brave boy gone?"

Finally, if we dig even deeper, beneath the meanings we associate with our needs, we find the emotional convictions that result. These are the devastating feelings about ourselves that accompany the message that our needs are "repulsive, weak, ugly, or selfish". This is the point at which our fence of denial sits, shielding us from the crushing feelings beyond. In front of this boundary stands the guardian of shame. Shame, with its annihilating force, attempts to protect us from the unbearable feelings that result from our rejections, abandonments, and our stories of self-blame. However, beyond this wall, lies the deep sense we have of being unlovable, unworthy, and not good enough. Unfortunately, even when buried, these feelings weigh heavily on us, holding us back from connecting with the world like leaden chains.

Shame: The truth will set you free

Shame marks the boundary between the darkness of denial and the awareness that we allow ourselves to have. It is a smokescreen: a feeling so uncomfortable that it feels impossible to pass through. Shame can be felt in the body in various ways, such as a tingling energy, a tightening, pins and needles or as an overwhelming sense of dread. Through the intensely uncomfortable sensations that shame gives us, denial achieves its mission of preventing us from becoming aware of the unbearable perceptions and emotional convictions that lie beyond.

Whilst we may not be aware of the narratives and convictions that denial and shame hide from us, they are still alive in our subconscious minds, and we will therefore still act as if they are true. As a result, we live our lives as if we really are unlovable and unworthy, with all the heartbreaking consequences this entails, despite these emotional convictions being inaccurate and outdated. Whilst we could only cope in the past by blaming ourselves, as we mature, it becomes far more acceptable to acknowledge the shortcomings of our caregivers and doing so will not result in the unthinkable anxiety that it might have once created. The more accurate narrative—that it is the context we were in, not a personal deficit, that leads to unmet needs—is a liberating truth that can set us free. Shame, however, sets up a tragic stalemate by blocking off this path of discovery with its prohibitive force.

Our deepest and most fundamental needs belong to the very earliest and most dependent stages of our development. As a result, unmet needs and traumas from this vulnerable time in life are buried deepest in our subconscious, carrying the most shame and denial. Our dependency too can come to feel inseparably bound up with the taboo of our early needs, become a source of great shame in itself. We can spend our whole lives running from dependency, shame, and the feelings that it is guarding us from. Sadly, in doing so, we end up heading in the very opposite direction to what our deepest needs are calling for.

Substitutions and addictions

When our needs feel impossible to meet, we are forced to find other ways of coping. These are the compromises and workarounds that partner with our denial to get us by. For example, whilst Sarah from Chapter 1 needed to be related to with genuine interest in order to feel lovable, she had learnt, in the absence of this, that in taking care of others and establishing a likeable personality she could find an alternative sense of feeling valuable. However, in shaping herself to be what she thought other people wanted her to be, her need to feel appreciated for who she truly was could never properly be met. Instead, this need was shrouded in shame and denial, which concealed her true identity even from herself, protecting her from the threat of further rejection and the feeling of being unlovable. In this way, the pain of her unmet needs was put on hold, and she was able to gain a feeling of control in being able to "make" people like her. In other words, she did her best to try and meet this need for herself. Denial provides us with illusions of self-sufficiency as a bandage for the pain of our unmet needs, but ultimately limits us in our actual fulfilment of them.

Working alongside our denial and illusions of self-sufficiency are the other methods of self-regulating that we find in the world in order to cope. We search for substitutes that can soothe us without having to put ourselves in the exposed positions that our dependent needs would demand. Almost anything can become a source of psychological and emotional refuge: a hobby, a drug, an ideology, sex, validation from others, or anything that brings us comfort. When we find respite in this world, it is natural to want more. Often, though, these behaviours do not fully scratch the itches that initially lead us to seek refuge in the first place. Within the pains, discomforts, and empty spaces that we seek to soothe are the heartaches of profound longings. These deep hungers, desires, and yearnings can be understood as unmet developmental needs or simply appreciated as part of our human nature. They take many different forms: feeling seen as you truly are, to have the darkest places in you blessed with unconditional acceptance, to be supported where you feel most weak, and endless other varieties of deep hungers that are impossible to put into words. What they do have in common is that they are all longings that cannot be fulfilled without opening up to the world. Otherness, in one way or another, is needed. As we have discovered, this brings with it the threat of the exposure of our vulnerability. These are hungers that we cannot satisfy by feeding ourselves. They bring the threat of dependency, but they also bring the promise of what lies beyond ourselves. Unless we are deeply touched, we will never feel truly fulfilled, and we will always be left in need of solace.

When these longings are not met, it hurts. Being hungry is painful, and to have an unmet need is to suffer. To manage, we find comfort in the psychological refuges and coping mechanisms mentioned earlier, which allow us to be self-sufficient and to avoid the vulnerability of dependency. These adaptations are part of our human nature and not something that we should see as shortfalls. When in balance, they can provide temporary relief and support when we need it. Sometimes, however, the adaptations that we make in order to seek comfort from our pain actually end up bringing us more suffering, leading to a gathering momentum of dysregulation. Whilst we may be trying to protect ourselves by avoiding the vulnerability of our dependency, by denying it we can actually lose touch entirely with our needs and deepest longings. When we find ourselves desperately seeking satiation, but do not let ourselves know the source of our own hunger, our behaviour can be a source of painful confusion.

When our attempts to self-soothe are hidden beneath our conscious awareness, it is easy to lose control of them. In going underground, the methods we hope to find regulation in become themselves destabilising. Unfortunately, the loss of autonomy and control that this can bring leads to further feelings of shame. What was meant to be a self-sufficient adaptation to avoid a dependent need ends up being a source of dependency itself. Our inner attitudes and those of society towards dependency can contribute to the shame that this dependency brings, making this vicious cycle even harder to break. Denial and shame become themselves sources of further denial and shame, and the witnesses that need to be killed off multiply out of our control. Our shame and denial really are convinced that there is a murder that needs to be covered up somewhere: something truly terrible that needs to stay hidden at all costs. The heartbreaking truth is, there really is nothing to be ashamed of. Our addictions are simply the ways in which we are trying to survive this difficult life by attempting to protect the tenderness of our own needs and heart's desires from the world. What we are trying to avoid at all costs is the wound that lies at the centre of it all, the deeply held conviction that we are somehow unlovable, bad or unworthy. The good, but tragic news, is that this is essentially just a big misunderstanding.

In Alcoholics Anonymous, the first of the twelve steps towards sobriety is "We admitted we were powerless over alcohol—that our lives had become unmanageable".[7] To embrace powerlessness and dependency cuts off shame and denial from the source of its power and ends their vicious cycle. It is not shameful to seek comfort and support. The ways in which the world has let us down are not our shortfalls to carry. In accepting dependency, we are less trapped by the confines we create for ourselves when we try to avoid it. Free from a fear of being powerless in our need for others, we are able to drink more deeply from the sustenance that our connection to the world can give us. In being very honest with ourselves, daring to descend beneath our shame, we have the possibility of really knowing our hearts and meeting the world with our deepest longings and needs. To surrender to dependency and powerlessness is to be open to the power of our early dependent states. Babies might be physically powerless, but to see the world from the raw and vital perspective of early life is to be in touch with new, creative possibilities. It is to let life flow more freely in and out of us again. To embrace our dependency is to open up to the world, surrendering our illusions of control, self-sufficiency, and independent separateness.

"My problems are nothing"

Embracing powerlessness and vulnerability is not easy. The denial of our unmet needs and dependency is deeply ingrained in us and can influence us without our knowledge. This can manifest itself in intimate relationships as unexpected outbursts of anger, arguments, a numbness to emotion, and in other ways that we will explore in the next chapter. In addition to these dramatic manifestations, the defensive function of this denial can be observed in small everyday moments. An example of this that occurs time and time again in my consulting room is when somebody says, "Compared to other people's problems, mine are nothing." Often, a client will say this just as they are starting to really open up to me about something particularly difficult or moving. It is frequently said with a slight air of contempt towards the "navel-gazing attitude of psychotherapy". This is said as a sudden U-turn to opening up. Within this self-interrupting statement is the structure of an important psychological defence mechanism that is key to understanding the impact of denying dependency.

Much of the process of psychotherapy is trying to understand and uncover meaning in all the little things that happen in a session: the idea is that all the templates and maps that we have built up over the years to understand and make sense of the world are all online and active at any given moment. Much like the pair of glasses in the first chapter, these maps remain hidden before our very eyes. Behind each feeling, belief, and interaction, these programmes are always at work. Therefore, by understanding a small moment of experience in great detail, it is possible to peel away the layers and glimpse the increasingly more fundamental lens and maps through which we see the world.

When we dig beneath the surface of the phrase "Compared to other people's problems, mine are nothing," what can be learnt about the deeper meanings behind this sentiment? What is the client really saying and why? The meaning for each individual may vary considerably. After all, we all have different histories, experiences, and characters that influence how we see the world. But, in generalised terms, a client will say this due to a sudden self-consciousness of their own vulnerability as they begin to open up. Just as they are about to depend on someone, to share their difficult feelings, a sense of shame and fear of let-down is triggered. The vulnerable act of reaching out to be held and soothed in the arms of another is suddenly retracted. By saying "Compared to other people's problems, mine are not that bad," a rejection of their request to be cared for is pre-empted. In doing so, the client is protecting themselves from the vulnerability that comes with opening up: they are avoiding re-experiencing the feelings that came with the initial rejection of their dependent need. This is why advice, or trying to fix someone's problem, often goes down so badly when somebody is opening up. It can be experienced as a snub to the request to be looked after. To be told "Don't worry, it's not that bad" or "This is how you can fix it" can feel like the equivalent of being given the message "Don't give me your difficult feelings, here's how you can look after yourself." It can feel like being told that their request to depend on someone else is actually unwelcome: a profound rejection of their sensitive vulnerability.

Why would a client in therapy be afraid that the therapist is going to dismiss their problems? Surely this is unrealistic? It is very true that most of the time in therapy, when a good relationship has been established, most clients will experience their therapists as an understanding and non-judgemental presence. Which is why, as trust builds, unmet needs from the past resurface with the hope that perhaps they can now be met. Could this be somewhere they can finally find the care that they really need from someone else? However, as this hope surfaces, it also brings the threat of re-exposing the client to the feelings that come with the rejection of their reaching out. This is not a conscious thought, but rather the expression of the subconscious fear: the lesson that they have learnt that their need for someone else is either unwanted or impossible to meet. Because of this, a person offering care and support can actually appear incredibly threatening: they represent the exposure of the client's vulnerability. When this protective mechanism kicks into full swing, both the person offering care and their inner vulnerability are attacked in order to keep the threat of dependency at bay. This is known as "self-sabotaging".[8]

Fight not flight

"Self-sabotage" is as much about sabotaging our own needs as it is about attacking whatever it is that has awoken our vulnerability. Before we explore its impact on our relationships in the next chapter, let us first consider the effects that this attack has on us as individuals and as a society.

Where being strong, self-sufficient, or tough is part of our identity, there is an increased need to suppress our own vulnerability and therefore a greater requirement to attack anything that threatens to expose it. When feeling or expressing vulnerability is not an option, the ways in which we can interpret experiences and express emotion are greatly limited. This is especially true in situations that evoke vulnerable feelings. For example, if you cross the road and nearly get hit by a car, most people will experience a huge surge of fear and adrenaline. However, when being scared feels like being weak and therefore unacceptable, the flood of adrenaline that is felt needs to be interpreted and expressed in a different way than fear. Often, the replacement is anger. Sometimes anger is necessary in these "fight" or "flight" situations and can usefully serve us as a protective force. However, when "fear" never feels permissible, the only acceptable response left to us will be to "fight". This takes the element of choice and freedom out of the situation, and we become unable to act effectively and appropriately in relation to the context. This does not just apply to emergency "fight" or "flight" situations. This same process can occur any time that any unwanted feelings of vulnerability are felt. On each occasion, the emotional intensity of the vulnerable state, whether that is fear, upset, grief, insecurity, or loneliness, gets channelled into an "acceptable" expression that is not in conflict with an identity that needs to be strong at all times. So often this "acceptable" expression ends up being anger, as it serves the dual function of both expressing the emotional affect and also of attacking and suppressing the source of whatever has awoken the underlying vulnerability.

When it feels unacceptable to show vulnerability, it can force us into some very tight corners. This contributes to many common phobias and anxieties, such as social anxiety and a fear of public speaking. Being seen as anxious, and therefore vulnerable, becomes itself a source of shame and anxiety. Needless to say, this causes further anxiety, and soon a downward spiral can be set in motion. When worry or anxiety feels so taboo to our own sense of self that we do not acknowledge to ourselves that we are feeling anxious, we may even interpret this panic as a physical phenomenon such as heart palpitations, chest pains, or dizziness. Again, the power of this process all hinges on the denial of vulnerability. Where vulnerability becomes acceptable, being seen as anxious ceases to be a cause for anxiety itself and social situations and public speaking can again become normal causes of regular nervousness.

Big boys don't cry

For men, expressing vulnerability can be particularly difficult. This is especially true in cultures where the narratives that exist around masculinity are particularly narrow and inflexible. When being a "real man" is defined in very limited terms, such as being powerful, unemotional, and independent, the vulnerability and dependency that are such vital and ever-present features of life need to be constantly denied in order to maintain a sense of masculine identity. As a result of the extent of this denial, masculinity exists in a constant state of fragility and subconscious anxiety (that is itself denied). Sadly, the defence against this anxiety comes at a great cost to both men and the rest of society.

Whilst there is certainly a cultural layer to this element of male identity, perhaps there is also a developmental one. When growing up, boys are usually not of the same gender as their primary caregiver: a mother. Therefore, when developing a sense of "self" and "other", the sense of separateness that comes with forming a sense of self can become inextricably linked to male identity. Maleness therefore becomes synonymous with separateness and the foundations of selfhood. Being merged and dependent as a baby belongs to a time prior to this separate male identity being developed, leaving dependency and "merged togetherness" feeling as though they fundamentally contradict male identity. As a result of this, when a man's male identity feels under threat, it can feel to them as though their entire sense of a separate self is at risk, contributing to further anxiety. In a culture of "toxic masculinity", one of the only acceptable ways that a man can express a need for another is as a sexual desire for women. The vulnerable, dependent needs of being held, touched, soothed, and comforted, all get channelled into sexual longings. Losing this sense of separate self in merger, therefore, becomes both the greatest fear and the secret longing of masculine identity.

In cultures where men do not feel as though they can express vulnerability, they will struggle to get close to others, as opening up is synonymous with being vulnerable. Furthermore, this "toxic masculinity" also makes male identity more fragile, which leads to ever-increasing levels of denial and anxiety that end up being defended offensively. Just like the process of "self-sabotage", anything that threatens to expose this vulnerability is viciously attacked. This contributes to misogyny, transphobia, and attacks on sexual and gender fluidity, as rigid conceptions of masculinity leave no room for flexibility or inclusivity.[9] A more nuanced and fuller story of masculinity is needed that does not define masculinity in opposition to vulnerability, but instead embraces it as part of a whole. Being able to tolerate feelings of powerlessness, dependency, and our need for others is very challenging and could even be seen as a powerful capacity. However, it would be even better if vulnerability could be accepted within male identity without having to frame it in terms of being "powerful" first. When masculinity can incorporate a wider diversity of qualities, it will no longer be such a narrow knife-edge to walk. Furthermore, when maleness is not based on superiority, stepping off this edge will not be a fall or step downward and therefore cease being a cause for anxiety.

Killing our caregivers

As babies, we all looked to our early primary caregiver, usually a mother, as an omnipotent God who we are at the loving mercy of. Both as individuals and as a society, the defences we build against dependency are maintained by attacking anything that reminds us of or threatens to take us back to the powerlessness of our early dependency. Women can therefore become targets for the assassin of denial that wants to take out all the witnesses to our dependency. In particular, feminine power, which is reminiscent of a mother's omnipotence, is suppressed and attacked, contributing to sexism and misogyny. However, just as women are attacked for representing someone who can take care of all our needs, they are also demonised for not being able to meet them all too. Many cultures have narratives of femininity that require women to be infallible caregivers, meeting everyone else's needs, but not having any of their own. In this way, women's dependent needs are also denied, which can make it more difficult for women to identify, express, and meet their own need for others.

Whilst culture is largely responsible for this attack on women, perhaps there is also a developmental contribution. To an infant, the realisation that their mother is not there solely to look after their needs dawns on them through their experience of their mother's own agency. This brings with it the realisation of their dependency, triggering vulnerable and difficult feelings. This is often too much for the infant to process, and they resort to "self-sabotage" for the first time. Rather than being able to process the difficult feelings of powerlessness and vulnerability that they are experiencing, they feel outrage towards their mother, attacking the source of care that has triggered their unbearable feelings. Just as the process of "self-sabotage" is taken through to adulthood, so too perhaps are feelings of outrage towards women's autonomy.

Whether this is a purely cultural phenomenon or if there is a developmental contribution, it is difficult to say. Either way, we live in a world where women's autonomy is repressed, denied, and feared to various extents. This is particularly evident when it comes to how women's sexuality is treated in a patriarchal society. Patriarchy offers men the narrative that it is women's autonomy and sexuality that is evil, so that they do not have to deal with their own feelings of vulnerability, such as abandonment, jealousy, insecurity, inadequacy, or powerlessness that they may face when women are not under their control. Blaming women provides an alternative outlet of hatred for these feelings, giving men an "out", where they do not have to learn to cope with and take responsibility for their own vulnerability. A modern example of this is the issue of "body count": the number of people that one has had sex with. It is a common talking point of the alt-right, where there is a narrative that says women who have slept with a lot of people are of less value. This is a clear example of "self-sabotage". In this case, women and their sexuality are attacked, despite being what these men deeply long for, in order for them to avoid having to confront the possibility of feeling inadequate, inferior, or insecure when they imagine that they might be being compared to other lovers.

The picture that is painted of what a woman is, or should be, needs to be expanded and enriched far beyond its current image, which focuses on a woman's capacity to look after others. Femininity, like masculinity, needs to be an identity that can provide us with shelter, should we choose to adopt it. Choice is the important point. An identity that is thrust upon us, without our choosing, is a cage, not a home. Lastly, when vulnerability can be embraced by society and culture, sexism and misogyny will diminish, as feminine power is only feared to the same extent that vulnerability and dependency are.

Summary

As we grow up, we learn through personal experiences of being let down and cultural messages that not all the needs we have for others are welcome. When we are unable to find what we need in our relationships with others, we face a hopeless dilemma that we cannot move on from. This is trauma. Denial partners with shame and fabricates stories to fence off the wounds of our unmet needs and hide from us the emotional convictions that we develop about ourselves as a result of not having our needs met. There is tragedy in this, as we often unfairly blame ourselves, feeling a sense of shame that prevents us from discovering that the accusations that we level at ourselves are actually unfounded. When these buried, unmet needs are triggered and fear wins over hope, we deny the vulnerable feelings stirred inside and instead attack whoever is offering us care. When being vulnerable is not possible, there are disastrous consequences for the individual and society, such as addiction, anger, fragile and toxic masculinity, misogyny, and sexism. A new relationship to vulnerability must be forged.

CHAPTER 4

Relationships

In our closest relationships, our vulnerability faces its greatest challenges. Allowing ourselves to unreservedly want and need somebody can leave us feeling profoundly exposed, making even minor disturbances in these relationships feel like colossal threats. To protect ourselves from the vulnerability of feeling completely at the mercy of another, denial steps in, leaving us tangled in webs of anger, jealousy, numbness, and avoidance. As we try to keep ourselves safe, we not only find ourselves cutting off from the relationships that are most precious to us, but also exiling the parts of ourselves that most need support. Relationships can feel like a confusing whirlwind at times, but by understanding our most fundamental need for others, we can begin to make sense of the turbulence we go through, finding joy instead of pain.

Kaitlin

To better understand how denial affects our relationships, let us follow one of my clients through her journey of psychotherapy. Kaitlin was a successful businesswoman in her early 30s with a vast array of achievements to her name. However, in the last five years Kaitlin had been feeling increasingly isolated and yearned for a long-term partner with whom she could share her life. However, most of her relationships seemed to end not long after they started, usually with heated arguments. Kaitlin explained how she often struggled with feelings of intense jealousy, which she felt very ashamed of. She had grown up in what she described as a "happy childhood", despite her parents divorcing when she was a teenager. When we first met, she described herself as being very independent, and when asked if she ever felt powerless in relationships she paused and replied, "No, that's the funny thing, I always feel like I'm the one in control."

The following dialogue portrays one particular moment, towards the beginning of our therapy, where Kaitlin was just starting to get in touch with the vulnerable feelings that lay beneath her jealousy. She began by describing to me an argument that she had experienced over the weekend with her new partner, George. She had been with George for a few months now and was increasingly hopeful and excited for the future of their relationship. They had just spent a sunny afternoon in the park, laughing and enjoying each other's company. She had even spoken to George about her father, who had left her family in her early teenage years, a conversation she had not had with anyone else outside of therapy. Later that evening, after having a nice meal, George said he was tired and wanted an early night, to which Kaitlin replied "Fine, I think I'm going to go home." An argument then followed, the details of which she struggles to remember.

In her session with me, Kaitlin and I explored together the moments in the lead-up to the argument.

Client—Kaitlin (K) and Therapist—Joseph (J)

K: I guess, thinking about it now, I can see how I felt mad that he'd stayed up with his workmates last week, and now, here he is, wanting to go to bed at 9 o'clock!

J: Maybe wondering "Why does he not want to stay up with me?"

K: Yeah … I guess we'd been having such a lovely day up until that point … it just felt so sudden.

J: Like suddenly he wasn't going to be there?

K: Yeah … but all I could think of in that moment was how he's probably sleeping with his workmate behind my back. I know he's not, though … it's strange. I didn't want to blow up the relationship by bringing that up … I know it's a bit crazy.

J: Like you were really angry in that moment … but also felt like you had to really try and hold that in, or it would hurt the relationship.

K: Yeah, and I didn't want to seem like a psycho. As the argument went on, I guess I realised more how angry I was, which only made things worse. Urgghh … (*She lets out a distressed sigh with a look of disgust on her face. A long silence follows.*)

J: I'm wondering whether maybe something feels hard to say … or feel even, in this moment?

K: Yeah … (*Another silence follows. Kaitlin has her arms folded and is looking down at herself. It looks as though she is trying to disappear.*)

J: What's it like telling me about this?

K: I guess I feel like you're going to think I'm a psycho too.

J: Like maybe there's a danger here too?

K: Not a danger, no … (*A silence follows. Kaitlin is sitting more upright now. I feel some anxiety stirring and find myself wondering if my use of the word "danger" was a step too far.*)

J: A judgement perhaps?

K: Yeah, although I know you therapists aren't supposed to judge. (*I feel a jolt as she says the word "therapist" and suddenly feel quite far away. The brewing intensity in the room has dissipated, and Kaitlin looks more composed now.*)

J: Yeah … that makes sense … to not feel like opening up if you feel you might be judged.

K: I mean, I don't really think you'll judge me, it's just a worry that if you were to see me as I really am … then … I don't know.

At this point, both in the therapy session and in her relationship with George, Kaitlin is just beginning to connect with the fear of abandonment that arises when she feels close to someone. This was a particularly difficult time for Kaitlin, as she was stuck right in the middle of her hope and fear, torn between opening up and protecting herself. Previously, she had kept herself at a safe distance by either avoiding relationships or "sabotaging" the start of any relationship that promised intimacy and closeness. However, Kaitlin was now allowing herself to become vulnerable and, in doing so, had to face her fears of abandonment and the protective habits that seemed poised to threaten her relationships.

In order to illustrate the process of Kaitlin's "self-sabotage" more fully, I will narrate my imaginings and interpretations about what might have been going on inside her during her argument with George. When faced with the "micro-abandonment" of George going to bed early, Kaitlin's protective system goes on to high alert. The priority for this system is to deny Kaitlin's vulnerable need for George in order to safeguard her from abandonment and the feelings of rejection and worthlessness this brings. This is a process that happens mostly beneath her conscious awareness; instead, her denial constructs an alternative narrative about how it is George who is being unreasonable by going to bed early. This allows her to make sense of her outrage and, at the same time, avoid connecting with her feelings of vulnerability. For Kaitlin, the vulnerable feelings that she is denying are particularly unbearable as they resonate with previous traumatic experiences of abandonment that she has not yet been able to process. As a result, any feelings of abandonment and rejection, no matter how small, feel totally unmanageable and impossible to acknowledge. We return to the subject of processing trauma in Chapters 8 and 9; however, for now, let us continue exploring Kaitlin's defensive response.

Kaitlin's denial did not stop there; it goes one step further, developing into a full-blown narrative of "self-sabotaging" jealousy. She tells herself that maybe George is being unfaithful: an explanation that justifies leaving him, which would ensure her safety. After all, you cannot be abandoned if you leave the other person first. The emotions that are triggered subconsciously by this "micro-abandonment", such as Kaitlin's despair and grief, are not fully felt or expressed, but channelled into a jealous anger. This then presents her with a further psychological predicament: that by displaying her anger, she is showing that she does really care about George, thus exposing her vulnerability further. This leads to further waves of "self-sabotage" and denial. Kaitlin is caught in a downward spiral: her denial is bursting at the seams, and her protective "self-sabotaging" system is on overdrive, struggling to keep her vulnerability safely hidden and screaming at her to push George away and retreat from the relationship. Yet Kaitlin does not do so. She did not accuse him of sleeping with his work colleague and was able to remain present in the relationship without fully retreating. This is because she is beginning to learn to identify, tolerate, and feel her shame, fear, and vulnerability. Consequently, in having some awareness of the "self-sabotaging" impulses of her protective system, she is not entirely swept away with them.

Microcosm

Kaitlin's argument with George is only half the story. The interaction between Kaitlin and me in the therapy room equally demonstrates the way in which she has learnt to keep her vulnerability safe, although at a much lower emotional intensity. Before we explore this further, let us explore the role that the relationship between client and therapist has in psychotherapy.

In therapy, the client and therapist have the unique opportunity to both participate in and analyse their relationship in real time as they experience it. This gives rise to two important aspects of therapy. First, by exploring and reflecting on the nuances of the interactions that occur between therapist and client, the underlying templates, beliefs, and patterns that inform the client's experience of their relationships may be revealed. These maps and meanings, whilst learnt in past relationships, are all alive, active, and therefore knowable in the present. In other words, the relationship between the client and therapist is an explorable microcosm of all the past relationships that the client has been a part of.[10] In addition to this, therapy can be a place where a client experiences a different way of being related to. Of particular importance are instances where the therapist is able to provide a relational environment that allows a client's previously banished feelings, needs or experiences to emerge, giving the client the opportunity to process them.

For Kaitlin, therapy became a place where she could become aware of her own protective mechanisms. The safety of the therapy arrangement allowed her to feel the threat of abandonment, all the while knowing that, on some level, she was safe: that I was going to remain present with her both physically and psychologically. As her awareness grew, she became more cognisant of how the same process that she described occurring with George, of becoming fearful of being abandoned and then pushing him away, were also happening in the therapy room with me. In the dialogue shared earlier, she was able to get in touch with her fear of judgement: a proxy for her fear of abandonment. However, when I suggested there she perhaps felt something "dangerous", I pushed her too far, too soon, towards her fear of abandonment. In response, she retreated back into her shell, pushing me away and protecting her vulnerability by reminding herself of the distance and safety that came with thinking of me as a professional and detached "therapist". Despite this mild attack, I remained open and responsive to Kaitlin. This allowed her the freedom of being able to explore the feelings that came up for her in these challenging moments, without having to worry that her protective "self-sabotaging" would lead to her abandonment. With the support and safety of this more emotionally regulated environment, she was able to increasingly connect with the vulnerable feelings beneath, learning to feel and process them without resorting to "self-sabotage". Kaitlin's therapy did not end there, and we will pick up her story again in Chapter 9 to follow the rest of her journey in integrating her vulnerability.

Attachment

We all need someone to look after us, whether it is the moment-to-moment attentiveness required during infancy or the support of a partner or friend through a difficult time. Tragically, however, someone else is not always there when we need them. This is one of life's most difficult experiences: whether it be the loss of a lover, the death of a parent, or simply a moment of sadness with no one there to comfort us. Even our birth may be imagined as a traumatic separation from a supportive other. We have all had to face the challenges of loss. How then do we navigate the emotional bonds that we have with others, knowing that we will inevitably face let-down and absence?

How we approach relationships and manage separation, aloneness, and our need for others varies from person to person. A popular way of talking about these different approaches to managing this in our relationships with others is the concept of "attachment". Attachment describes the quality of the bond of a relationship. Attachment theory originates mainly from the work of Mary Ainsworth and John Bowlby, and an experiment called the "strange situation".[11] In the "strange situation" experiment, infants were put in a room alongside their mothers and a stranger and their behaviour was closely observed. The mother leaves the room and, after a short while, returns. The behaviour that the infant displays was then used to determine their "attachment style", which was classified as either "secure", "insecure avoidant", or "insecure anxious". When an infant is securely attached, they freely explore the new environment in the presence of their mother, although they are moderately upset when she leaves the room and they are left in the presence of a stranger. When their mother returns, securely attached infants will seek her presence and find it easy to be comforted and soothed by her. Anxiously attached infants are fearful of straying too far from their mother to explore and are much more upset when their mother leaves. They are also much more difficult to comfort upon her return. Lastly, infants with an avoidant attachment style will freely explore the new environment and show no distress when their mother leaves and no interest in interacting with the stranger or reuniting with their mother when she returns. Ainsworth and Bowlby described how these different attachment styles are then carried into adult relationships, resulting in either a secure, anxious, or avoidant style of attachment.

Attachment styles have found their way into everyday language and can be very useful ideas for identifying and understanding the way in which we relate to others. Like any theory, however, it also carries the potential to simplify and reduce a more complex and nuanced matter to something that is a fraction of its greater nature. Whilst attachment styles are commonly thought of as fixed types, it is important to keep in mind that they can change over years, months and even from moment to moment depending on the context or relationship.[12] Ainsworth originally suggested that the quality of attachment an infant develops is determined by the mother's responsiveness: appropriate responsiveness fosters secure attachment, unresponsiveness or absence leads to avoidant attachment, and inconsistent responsiveness results in anxious attachment. Whilst Ainsworth was concerned with the formative quality of the mother–infant relationship, it is helpful to keep in mind that responsiveness is an ongoing process that can impact our feeling of security moment to moment in all our relationships, not just with our primary caregiver. When you are in a relationship with someone who is inconsistent, absent, or unresponsive, it is hard for anybody to feel secure. This is just as true for our external relationships as it is for our inner ones, something we will explore shortly.

A helpful way of understanding attachment styles is to look at them, as the psychotherapist Bruce Tift does, as relating to the fundamental qualities of togetherness and separateness.[13] He describes how an anxiously attached person will move towards the other person in order to seek regulation and safety within the state of togetherness. On the other hand, an avoidantly attached person will take a step back in order to find regulation and safety in their separateness. He goes on to say how we often seek out a partner with the opposite style, subconsciously trying to find balance, but without having to change our attachment style. This allows us to avoid confronting the underlying dynamics of our relationship style and the traumas that may lie beneath it. In all relationships, the space in between is constantly changing: in one moment, there is close togetherness and in the next, a distance and separateness. Relationships can be thought of like a dance, where the connection between partners is expressed in the flow and movement between them. Whilst togetherness can often feel like the goal of a relationship, separateness is equally important, providing the quality of "otherness", without which togetherness is simply merging.

Dancing can lose its joy when we do not feel as if we can move freely and have become trapped in a dance routine that does not feel like a true expression of ourselves. Returning to "attachment" theory, it is helpful to realise that because our relationship with our primary caregiver goes on to become our most influential and habitual template of relating to others, we tend to enter our adult lives having learnt only the movements that helped us regulate the relationship with this one specific person. Where our primary caregiver regulated and responded to the "space in between" sensitively, we are likely to have learnt a wider variety of movements and built a greater capacity for regulating the distance in-between. However, if our caregiver was always moving away, we would have learnt that moving forwards is always necessary. In fact, moving forwards will probably come to feel as natural as standing still and yet all the time we will be unknowingly taking steps towards those around us. In response, others are likely to take steps backwards, not to retreat, but merely to maintain a steady distance. On the other hand, if our caregiver was always moving forward, we would probably have learnt that we always need to move backwards in order to avoid a proximity that is not too close (which can feel overwhelming). When attachment is disturbed like this, relationships can feel like a distressing chase, leaving us either feeling constantly abandoned or in fear of being engulfed by our partner. When we grow up learning that either moving forwards or backwards is always necessary, we lose the capability for the opposite movement and its corresponding capacity for independence or dependence. This disrupts the dance of our relationships and hampers our ability to find regulation in them.

Luckily, our attachment and relationship styles are not done deals. In fact, it is quite common in my experience for clients to change their attachment style during the course of therapy. For example, somebody like Kaitlin, who has related mostly in an avoidant fashion in the past, transitioned into having more experiences of feeling anxiously attached during the early stages of the psychotherapy process. For many clients like Kaitlin, the responsive environment of psychotherapy awakens unmet needs that lie beneath a person's avoidant or anxious style of attachment. When Kaitlin learnt to be self-sufficient in the absence of a suitably supporting relationship (during the trauma of her parents' divorce, but also possibly at an earlier developmental point in her relationship with her mother too), she buried her need for others and developed a more avoidant style of relating, turning towards herself, and maintaining distance in her relationships for security. As her need for a relationship re-emerged, so too did her fear of rejection and abandonment. She therefore became uncomfortable, rather than reassured, by separateness and space in relationships. For Kaitlin, uncovering her buried need for others and relating in a more anxiously attached style is actually a step towards processing her trauma and developing a more secure attachment style.

Conversely, for somebody who starts off with an anxious attachment style, they would already be well acquainted with their need for others, but less familiar with their capacity to find regulation in separateness. This is because, to begin with, an anxious attachment style tends to develop in a context where stepping back from their caregiver would have meant too much absence. In this early relationship, independence would have therefore been experienced as a dysregulating aloneness. For someone with an anxious attachment style, getting in touch with their disconnected autonomy is the first challenging step towards a more secure attachment. When they finally do get in touch with their previously suppressed independence, it can feel very easily threatened. Closeness may feel as though it could overwhelm or destroy their newfound sense of self. They may find it difficult to be intimate with others without having very rigid boundaries in order to maintain their separateness. For this person, this transition, into what is effectively an avoidant style of attachment, is part of their process of learning how to find regulation in their separateness. It is therefore a move towards a more balanced and secure attachment. Regardless of the starting point, embracing a new way of relating is challenging, as it involves confronting the trauma of either the overwhelm or abandonment that their initial relational style had resolved.

Separateness and togetherness are two necessary facets of relationships that can feel like polar opposites that are hard to reconcile. At times, we deny one of these two halves and get stuck in a dysregulating relational pattern. Holding the tension of these "opposite" capacities and therefore being in touch with our ability to be both independent and dependent, is important in allowing our relationships to flow joyfully and freely. Relating from this balanced perspective is often referred to as relational interdependence. Interdependence, as we will discover later, is the paradox that lies at the heart of how all things are connected to each other. The dance of our human relationships brings alive this wonderful, yet often painful, mystery.

Abandoning ourselves

An important consequence of our denial of dependency is that when we disconnect from our need for others, we abandon a part of ourselves that requires support. What does "a part of ourselves" actually mean? Whilst we commonly experience ourselves as separate, distinct, continuous, and unitary beings, many schools of psychotherapy and some evidence from modern neuroscience point towards the self being made up of multiple independently operating "selves".[14] These "independent selves" can be thought of as parts of our personality, comprising clusters of different states of mind and feeling. It is as though we are actually like houses in which many different characters all live under one roof. With this cacophony of different voices, we weave together one singular and seamless tapestry, the narrative of our self. However, looking closely, it is the manner in which these threads are woven together that shapes us: the relationships within this internal community are the lifeblood of our selves. How we relate to our dependency is therefore an alive and ongoing relationship. When we reject our vulnerability, we are actually enacting an inner abandonment. To illustrate this, I will tell a story that takes place in a house.

> A little boy falls over and hurts his knee. He starts to cry and runs to find his daddy in the study. His father looks at him with concern, worried that his son is not going to survive in this world. "You need to toughen up!" he tells his son. The little boy pauses for a moment, lip trembling, before bursting into tears once more. The father loses his temper. "Go to your room and don't come out until you've stopped crying." When the little boy comes out of his room, he is no longer crying and will one day tell his own son to toughen up.

Stories may resonate beyond our intellectual understanding of the world, transcending past, present, and future, and straddling both inner psychological worlds and outer material ones. When we try and make sense of a story, inevitably something is lost in our understanding, and our interpretations only diminish a greater truth. Having said this, for the purposes of illustrating the concept of inner relationships, this story can be read as a snapshot of an internal process: the boy and his father are inner figures that make up a self. A person who tries to grow out of, transcend, or reject their vulnerability lives each moment with a child who is crying all alone, locked away in their bedroom, away from their conscious awareness. It is no wonder that they are afraid of abandonment. In an attempt to protect themselves from the pain of abandonment, they banish their own vulnerability and dependency with denial, confirming the fear of abandonment and perhaps even re-enacting a historical trauma. There is hope, however. Our inner relationships are occurring in each moment between living parts of our being. So, whilst the little boy may still be crying on his own in his bedroom, it is not too late to go and comfort him.

Summary

When we deny our dependency, closeness can feel as though it threatens to uncover our hidden need for others and the pain that comes with it. When we try to cut ourselves off from our vulnerability, we banish a living part of ourselves that is in need of both an inner and outer relationship. In doing so, we inwardly abandon ourselves and therefore live with the constant anxiety that this brings. The denial of our dependent vulnerability can show up in relationships as an avoidant style of attachment, where we avoid putting ourselves in the vulnerable position of being close to another person. However, when we lose our capacity to move towards or away from others, to be both dependent and independent, we limit our ability to find regulation and joy in the dance of relationships.

CHAPTER 5

Identities of superiority

When others let us down, we may end up feeling that it is our fault and that we are unworthy of love. One of the ways in which we try to cope with this hidden feeling of inferiority is to work relentlessly at trying to become "good enough". If only we can be successful enough, good-looking enough, kind enough, clever enough, then we will never again have to face our feelings of inadequacy or rejection. However, when we try to be better than we are, we enter into an impossible and fruitless struggle of denial. Not only does this have a detrimental impact on our relationships, but it also leads us into a vicious cycle of pushing others downwards in an attempt to climb higher. When we view the world in terms of superiority and inferiority, there are disastrous consequences for those around us.

Good enough

Self-worth is something that is nurtured in us by others. The esteem that we hold ourselves in is a reflection of the love that we have been shown by others, although not an exact replica of it. Just as we can emerge from loving childhoods with a sense of low self-worth due to tragic misunderstandings about our unmet needs, we can also find glimmers of love in even the harshest upbringings that, with nurturing, grow brighter over time. That being said, our feelings of self-worth are usually very closely related to the care that we have received from others. On the whole, where we have had our needs sensitively attended to, we feel a sense of being wanted by the world. Yet, even when our needs have been met, where they have been responded to in only a conditional manner, we can come to feel as though only a part of our being is worthy. For example, if we are only hugged when we are happy, it can feel as though our sadness is undesirable, and so we come to feel that part of our being is not welcome. Accepting and loving others unconditionally, whilst being a noble ambition, is impossible to embody, being the imperfect humans that we are. Therefore, in one way or another, we will all end up feeling as though, in some way, we are not "good enough" as we fully are.

One of the ways in which we try to cope with our low self-esteem is to try and earn our worth. Tragically, this strategy is doomed to fail. Being good enough will always remain a moving target. The emotional conviction that we are deficient in some way will not answer to facts or reason. It supersedes our rational minds, and no amount of evidence to the contrary will ever satisfy it. However much we strive and achieve, a hidden voice will always tell us that we are still not enough. "Good enough" will eternally dangle in front of us like a carrot on a stick, feeling just out of reach but nevertheless tempting us to chase its promises. Seeking reassurance of our value through our achievements, performance, or whatever other parameter we base this on is always going to leave us in a precarious position. Conditional acceptance is never going to give us the feeling of security that we are truly seeking.

Trying to become "good enough" is, at its core, a way of trying to transcend vulnerability altogether. It is to vow to never put ourselves in a position where we may face the possibility of rejection and abandonment. In order to do this, we have to disown and abandon all the parts of ourselves that do not measure up to our standards of acceptability. The harder we try to disconnect from the parts of ourselves we think are not good enough, the more abandoned and insecure we will feel. As we strive to be better than we are, we internalise the message that our current condition is unacceptable, and therefore we will see even more reason to try and become better. This can be a vicious cycle that is hard to escape.

The parts of ourselves that we deem to be inadequate will always remain inseparable aspects of who we are. Just like the crying boy in the last chapter, we can lock away the people who live in the "house" of the self, but they will remain alive in our subconscious minds. In addition to contributing to our feelings of inadequacy and fears of abandonment, this denial *en masse* has further consequences. First, locking so many people away requires a huge amount of energy, as denial is an active ongoing psychological process. This can sap our energy and lead to feelings of depression and lifelessness. Furthermore, sometimes the prisoners we keep locked away will not succumb quietly to their fate. They will bang on the door and stage dramatic attempts at escape. This can cause constant anxiety as we are subconsciously aware that at any moment there could be a breakout that would expose us as the unlovable people that we think we truly are. Lastly, the parts of ourselves that we judge as inferior are often the aspects of ourselves that need and depend on others. They are our lifeline to the world and the means by which we can receive love and care. When we lock them away, we close off the possibility of finding the connections with the world that might deeply fulfil us.

Michael

Michael, a successful and outgoing doctor in his early 40s, came to therapy seeking help for a general sense of depression and ongoing relationship difficulties with his wife. He lived an incredibly busy life, juggling his time between his demanding career, family life, and cycling competitively. Michael never missed a session and was never late.

I soon found myself looking forward to my sessions with Michael. He was articulate, intelligent, and thoughtful. He seemed lively on the surface, although it seemed, at times, as if his positive demeanour was hard work to maintain. When he did begin to talk about his feelings, he would talk about them as though they belonged to somebody else and would often say "Ah, it's nothing" or "It's stupid to feel like that."

The first interaction that I am going to share from our therapy sessions illustrates a typical exchange between us during the early phases of the therapy. As you can see, my responses do not seem to help him open up or develop insight. Understanding the deeper causes of the counter-productive dynamic that this exchange demonstrates would, however, prove to be an essential turning point in our therapy.

Client—Michael (M) and Therapist—Joseph (J)

M: (*Michael had just finished describing an argument that had taken place the previous week with his wife.*) I don't know where it came from; I just totally lost my temper.

J: Perhaps you felt criticised or maybe even inadequate?

M: (*Michael pulls his head back, looking somewhat shocked.*) No … not that. I don't know why I was angry; it wasn't even a particularly important argument.

J: It sounds like it had quite an impact on you.

M: I wouldn't say impact … I've just been under a lot of stress at work, and it's got to go somewhere …

After some time of working with Michael, I noticed I was beginning to feel frustrated in our sessions and realised that I was finding it increasingly difficult to respond to him. Over the course of some months, my frustration grew, and I began to have the strange sensation of feeling as though I could not think of anything to say. I took this curious development to my supervisor:

Therapist—Joseph (J) and Supervisor (S)

J: It's a strange feeling. I find myself not knowing what to say … like anything I do say will hit a brick wall.

S: A brick wall?

J: Yeah, he won't let it in … it feels like he has to think of everything for himself … like it's a competition.

S: Does it feel like there's a sense of competition between the two of you?

J: Yeah … there's an undercurrent of that … (*a silence follows*). It feels like he rejects everything I say, and now I've reached a point where I don't know what to say at all. I could be anyone …

S: What's that like? To feel as though you could be anyone?

J: It feels like he's not really seeing me … like he doesn't need me … that I've got nothing to give … (*silence*). Hmmm …

S: Does that touch on some of your own story?

J: Yeah … something has just clicked into place. The feeling of aloneness, of not being able to reach out … that's what I'm feeling when I'm with him. That's all familiar to me. The feeling of not having anything to give too … of not feeling good enough. That really makes sense.

In reaching out to my supervisor for help and receiving her acceptance and understanding, I was able to connect with my own feelings of vulnerability that were coming up in my work with Michael. This helped me to realise that when I felt locked out by Michael and struggled to find something to say, I had felt inadequate as a therapist and fearful of criticism. Rather than being aware of these feelings of insecurity at the time, I had instead found myself denying them and striving to be a "good enough" therapist. For example, when I had suggested to Michael "Perhaps you felt criticised or maybe even inadequate?" I was trying to prove my value to him by coming up with a clever and insightful interpretation that would progress the therapy.[15] Michael understandably did not open up in response. He likely sensed the rejecting attitude I held towards my own feelings of inadequacy and subconsciously decided that it was therefore not safe for him to expose his vulnerability either. After this supervision session, it became clear to me where my own experiences had been overlapping with Michael's: where my own templates and emotional convictions were being activated in our work together. I realised that I found myself wordless, not only because Michael was locking me out, but because I was locking myself out. Without being open to my own vulnerability, I had become disconnected from how I truly felt and therefore from my own voice.

As psychotherapists, it is par for the course that our own past experiences and the way in which they shape how we see the world will arise and colour our perception of therapy and the clients we see. This is not something we can, or should, seek to transcend. It is inevitable and can actually be a useful asset to our work. The relational and emotional experiences that we have with our clients are a reflection of both ourselves and our clients. When we attend to, reflect on, and understand our own experience, it often ends up illuminating our understanding of the client too. In this instance, becoming aware of my feelings of inadequacy and fear of rejection allowed me to resonate more deeply with Michael's vulnerability. This resonance is similar to how, when a musical note sounds, it will start vibrating the strings of the same note in nearby instruments. This is not to say that my feelings and experiences are the same as Michael's, but rather that our own feelings can set the tone for listening with a deeper sense of empathy. By using our feelings as a kind of antenna, we can look to our own experience and ask, "I wonder if this might be similar to how my client is feeling?" With this in mind, I wondered whether Michael may also feel "not good enough" in our therapy. As I reflected on this, I could easily imagine how he might have been experiencing my interpretations as criticisms. For example, when I suggested that he may have *felt* inadequate, he might have heard, on some level, that I was implying that he *was* inadequate. With this understanding, Michael putting up a "brick wall" makes total sense, as he was merely protecting himself from my "attacks" on his self-worth.

After this supervision session, my experience in therapy with Michael changed. In feeling aware of my desire to seek his approval and demonstrate my worth as a therapist, I was able to resist acting out this impulse. Instead, I allowed myself to connect with the feelings of inadequacy and being locked out that I was both feeling myself and hearing Michael subtly express. In doing so, I felt much more able to perceive and respond to Michael's hidden vulnerability. I found myself replying in a simpler way, sensitively supporting his experience in the moment, much like my supervisor had with me. In response, Michael began to find his own vulnerability. He began increasingly to talk about a time in his life when he was nine years old and his mother had become severely ill. In the exchange below, Michael had just been describing how, when his mother was unwell, his father had been totally preoccupied with distress and how Michael had felt all alone.

Client—Michael (M) and Therapist—Joseph (J)

M: Realising now how I felt … so alone. It's so sad … It makes me want to cry, but … I just can't. (*Michael looks at the ground with a look of sunken defeat on his face.*)

J: Like you desperately want to, but at the same time something is holding you back?

M: Yeah … I feel it inside. Like, I really need to cry, but it's so hard to do with someone else here.

J: Perhaps there's a part of you on the inside that is already crying?

M: It's like he's there, crying in the corner … and I'm telling him, you can't do that. (*He looks distressed now.*)

J: Maybe it felt like you couldn't?

M: (*silence*) … There was no one there. Nothing I did seemed to make a difference.

J: Alone … that sounds terrifying … and heartbreaking.

M: It was … "stay strong" they'd say … I tried so hard … I never cried.

J: And yet you really needed to …

M: Yeah … (*His lips tremble as his eyes well up. He turns away. His arms are wrapped around his body, half holding himself and half holding himself back. He begins to sob more deeply as his arms drop to his sides.*)

In revisiting this difficult time in his life, Michael was able to get in touch with the feelings and emotions that he had experienced when his mother was ill, but had not been able to express. He realised that, in being told to stay strong during a moment when he so desperately needed comfort, he had felt a profound sense that his inner emotional experience was unwelcome. Michael was left with the belief that if he were to become upset, he would be letting everyone down. He came away from this experience feeling as though his emotional needs were a terrible shortcoming that he should try and overcome at all costs. He went on to describe how, after his mother's illness, he decided to become a doctor, hoping not only to cure his mother, but to "cure" his vulnerability too. In becoming ultra-competent and high-achieving, he had subconsciously hoped that he could "grow out of" and become "better than" his vulnerability and never need to rely on someone else again.

As Michael's therapy progressed, he became increasingly aware of his feelings of rejection and inferiority, which greatly helped him to understand the difficulties he was encountering in his relationship with his wife. He realised that when they spoke, he would interpret any feelings that she expressed, of being upset or unsatisfied, as personal failings.

Often, the only message that he took away from an argument was: "You are not good enough." Just as he had been fighting an internal battle against this feeling by striving to be good enough, he waged the same war outwardly too, feeling as though he had to constantly justify and prove himself. To see himself, or to be seen as, inferior or not "good enough" in any way, challenged the whole identity that he depended upon for his psychological survival. It is understandable that he felt such a fierce need to defend himself.

Although Michael had lived his whole life denying his vulnerability, therapy became a place where it began to feel acceptable, and he was therefore able to resurface. Michael shifted from talking about his vulnerability as if it belonged to someone else to expressing it as his own. He was able to embody the crying boy and his feelings of aloneness, rejection, and longings to be comforted and held. In doing so, he let his defences down, and I was able to be alongside him, behind the walls that had kept him safe by keeping others out. Without this barrier, the crying boy inside was able to receive the acceptance, understanding, and compassion that he needed. Michael could then internalise this experience, changing his own inner relationship to the crying boy inside, who came to feel less alone and "good enough" as he was.

Superiority

When feeling "good enough" means never feeling inferior, we find ourselves in a situation where we need to feel better than others just to feel acceptable. This creates a dangerous and fragile "identity of superiority". Take, for example, a tennis player who only feels acceptable to themselves and others when they win. In order to maintain the status quo of their identity as a winner, they will require a steady stream of "losers" to defeat. Pushing downwards becomes not just necessary to rise upwards, but essential for merely maintaining a sense of justifiable existence. When we define ourselves as being "superior" and our sense of self becomes tied to that identity exclusively, any experience to the contrary threatens to undermine our psychological stability and is therefore defended against as if our life depends on it. Winning becomes a matter of surviving rather than thriving. This is distinct from the kind of motivation that springs from a creative and free-willed ambition towards a goal or vision, where striving is not tied solely to the function of defending and maintaining an identity. In contrast, an identity based on "superiority" is based on the conviction that only when we are better than others are we acceptable and worthwhile. Feelings of inferiority, vulnerability, and dependency simply do not make the cut.

In day-to-day life, somebody with an identity based on superiority will need to "win" all the time. This sets up an inherent fragility, as being constantly victorious is impossible. An "alpha male" identity is a good example of this. When a man needs to feel like they are at the top of the pile in order to feel acceptable, he sets himself up with a monumental task. In order to feel okay, he will need to be better than everyone else, just to maintain a regular sense of self-worth. When it is only acceptable to be exceptional, a situation is created where everyone scrambles over each other in order to ascend, dominating, controlling, and diminishing others on the way. When only being "better than" is enough, there is simply not enough acceptance to go round.

The struggle for superiority is not always present in such overt ways. Take, for example, my experience with Michael and the quiet sense of competition that existed between us in the beginning. Looking back, I think that on some level I had believed that I was not a "good enough" therapist if I was not more intelligent than my client. I wonder too, whether Michael felt something similar: that in order to feel acceptable, he had to feel more intelligent than me. Whilst on the surface we were trying to work together, subconsciously our identities, feeling threatened, worked against each other in order to justify themselves. As is typical of a contest for superiority, it was a fruitless struggle, as there was not room for both of us to win. In the end, for both myself and Michael getting in touch with and accepting our own feelings of inferiority and vulnerability proved to be turning points for the flourishing of both our relationship and the therapy. Where feelings of inferiority can be accepted, and therefore come to feel acceptable, there will be no struggle for supremacy.

A culture of supremacy

Just as our personal identities can secretly rely on a sense of superiority, so can the narratives of our collective identities. That is to say, we may come to learn that our collective identity means that we are in some way better than other groups of people. This can be a process that happens almost entirely outside of our conscious awareness. As we have explored previously, we relate to the vast majority of our maps and templates subconsciously, including the tapestry of narratives, both personal and collective, that make up our identities. This patchwork is formed from all the different stories and messages that we have internalised from our culture and the world around us about what it means to belong to the different identities that we see ourselves as being a part of. We may therefore not be fully aware of all the stories that we tell about our own identities or those of others. In fact, we may not even necessarily approve of or be in agreement with these stories, especially if we have not consciously reflected on them before. Yet they may nevertheless make up part of the subconscious reference map with which we view the world.

Now, let us consider what the consequences are when one of our collective identities relies on a sense of superiority. As an example, let us consider "white identity" and its (more often than not) subconscious narrative of superiority. Many white people might say there is no such thing as "white identity", let alone that there is any assertion of superiority. This no doubt reflects the fact that for many white people, their "white identity" and the narratives that it taps into are subconscious. Nevertheless, this does not mean that such a story does not exist. This blind spot can persist by virtue of the spectacles of culture being so close to one's eyes that we are unaware that we are viewing the world through the lens of a story. Furthermore, as white people do not have to experience the jarring day-to-day impact of racism, they have the privilege of not needing to look at or be aware of the subconscious racism that is woven into Western culture. Lastly, what contributes to making this difficult to perceive for white people is a resistance to acknowledging the elements of superiority and racism that exist in "white identity". This is because most white people do not consciously hold racist ideologies or values, and therefore acknowledging the racism present in the collective narratives of white identity would feel as though it compromises their own identity. After all, an identity is a story that attempts to unify our narratives as well as present an acceptable self-image to the world. In order to deal with this difference between personal identity and the collective narrative of Western culture, "white identity" and the superiority that exists within it often end up being denied.

To illustrate how this narrative of superiority shows up in a day-to-day fashion, let us consider some responses to the Black Lives Matter movement. A common response amongst some white people was to reply, "White lives matter too." This response indicates a defensiveness that suggests that, to this person, in acknowledging that Black lives matter feels like their white identity is under attack. This is comparable to an "alpha male" who is unable to give his fellow men and women equal status without feeling as though his own identity is compromised. When we have an identity based on superiority, equality feels like a threat.

Identities that rely on a sense of superiority exist in many forms within the contexts of class, gender, sexuality, ability, nationality, neurodiversity, and in many other ways. In most cases, a similar dynamic exists: there is a majority with more privilege and power, who are less consciously aware of the stories that make up their identity and a minority, who by virtue of their difference are more conscious of the narratives that culture tells about these identities. There are many different configurations of the way in which these identities can overlap and the different impacts that this carries, referred to as "intersectionality".[16] We each have our own relationship to the collective stories of identity that our culture tells us and to the way in which our own identities are constructed in complex and unique ways. In order to understand the stories that we are all immersed in, it is important to listen to the perspectives from a diverse range of people so that we can uncover blind spots and reduce the perpetuation of harmful narratives of superiority.

Whilst superiority is mostly a subconscious aspect of an identity, there are those for whom embracing an identity of superiority can seem to offer an opportunity to reclaim feelings of self-esteem and power in the face of feelings of helplessness, powerlessness, and vulnerability. This can be a major component in the rise of fascism, where an identity of superiority is sold to a population struggling with powerlessness, at the expense of creating an external group that is seen as an inferior scapegoat. When feelings of powerlessness, vulnerability, and inadequacy have no place in an identity, there is no other option but to deny them and wage a war against them both inwardly and outwardly.

Summary

When we are let down by others, we often blame ourselves, feeling that our abandonment is due to the fact that we are not "good enough" in some way. When our attempts to find comfort in others have been rejected, it can come to feel as though needing others is itself inferior. Trying to better ourselves is a coping strategy that aims to fix our self-perceived shortfalls by becoming accomplished and self-sufficient enough that we will never have to face rejection again. When striving for achievement comes from this fundamentally defensive place, it always involves the self-rejection of our vulnerable selves and will therefore never make us feel "good enough" or secure. When we define our sense of self as being better than others, we set ourselves up with a fragile identity that requires constant I. This can also apply to the collective identities we relate to subconsciously, as when an identity defines itself on superiority, equality can come to feel like an attack. Before we follow the path to a fuller acceptance of ourselves and others, we will first explore the profound extent to which the rejection of our vulnerability divides us in the next chapter.

CHAPTER 6

Becoming divided

No matter how much we may try to discard the parts of ourselves that we would rather be without, they are here to stay. When we deny an aspect of ourselves, we do not get rid of it completely, but merely disconnect from it, losing touch with the fullness of our whole self in the process. The more divided we become internally, the more we see ourselves as separate from the world, and the harder it becomes to experience our connection to it. Becoming divided is not only a process that affects our personal psychology, but also influences the fundamental stories that underpin our culture. In order to understand this, we begin by tracing the evolution of our modern-day paradigm and seeing how it contributes to our split perception of the world. We then explore Jung's theories of the "Self" and projection: concepts that give us a way of comprehending wholeness and the processes by which we become divided.

A split perspective

Judging our surroundings is an intrinsic part of the human condition; we chase after what we perceive as good and avoid what we consider bad. We have evolved to pursue our desires and to retreat from the unpleasant sensations of fear, pain, and disgust. Our survival as a species has depended on learning to distinguish the many different aspects of the world around us, such as identifying which foods are nutritious, which are poisonous, and where the best places to hunt and rest are. Perceiving the world in this divided way and judging it accordingly has always been a part of our most basic instincts. However, the stories through which we view the world can either amplify our sense of division and judgement or help us to see beyond the distinctions of good and bad that we perceive. To understand how our modern perspectives shape our view of ourselves and the world, we must look back into our distant past and question some of our most foundational stories.

The biggest shifts in how we view the world can be traced back to the rise of civilisation and the advent of monotheistic religions that followed. Very broadly speaking, in prehistoric times, for Indigenous populations all over the world, divinity was located within the different elements of nature such as the sun, moon, ocean, sky, plants, trees, and animals. The sacred not only resided within the natural world but was inseparable from it. It is hard to imagine what the world looks like from this perspective because our fundamental cultural assumption is that there is a separation between the physical and spiritual. It is this very assumption that developed with the rise of monotheistic religion. When God became disassociated from the physical world around us, nature began to be seen as a fallen place, devoid of divinity, spirit, or value. The material world was seen only as a temporary and profane place, with everything of value belonging to the eternal afterlife beyond. Nature, along with our animal bodies, became the enemy of the holy. In this worldview, everything appeared split in two: good and bad, material and spiritual. The legacy of this split in our perception is still alive today and profoundly shapes how we see the world. Whilst in our modern materialistic paradigm, we may not see ourselves as spiritual beings anymore, our consciousness and intelligence have replaced spirit to become what now defines us as separate and superior to the world around us. Our modern outlook is based on the implicit understanding that "we", our conscious minds, reside inside our heads and that the material world "outside" is "other" and of less value. Not only does this contribute to a profound alienation from the world, but it also has allowed us to treat nature with contempt.[17]

As history has progressed, our mythologies have become more reductionistic, reflecting our increasingly sophisticated understandings of the individual aspects of the universe. However, this way of understanding the world, solely in terms of its component parts, comes at the expense of a fragmented perception that loses touch with an appreciation of the whole. To explore this, let us look at our modern cosmology and its story of creation.[18]

> Nothingness. The Big Bang. Massive expansion and chaos followed by millions of years of darkness. Matter starts to gather together and over colossal amounts of time, the stars form and so too does Earth. The process of life begins to gather momentum and as time goes on, evolution sees us marching towards ever increasing levels of sophisticated existence.

This modern creation story is a tale of transcendence and ascension: of splitting off from the parts of ourselves that we do not like. Darkness is cast off and left behind in the past, along with our animal nature and barbaric history. Instead, we see ourselves heading into a bright future where we place our hopes, not unlike the promise of an afterlife. When you contrast our perception of time as a linear process to many Indigenous cultures' circular notions of it, it becomes easier to understand how this may shape our sense of belonging, or not, to a greater whole. When time is viewed as being circular, tied to nature's cycles, the past is not something that we can be separate from. Everything returns, and we can leave no piece of our wholeness behind. When the ground beneath you is eternal, you cannot bury your rubbish in it under the illusion that you will never have to face it again.

It is, of course, difficult to fully grasp how these fundamental elements of our culture actually shape our day-to-day experience of how we see the world. They are so deeply entrenched and foundational to our perception that it is nearly impossible to imagine what life would look like without them. What would it actually *feel* like to look at the world as if time were circular? How might that change the way in which we act as individuals and as a society? This is not a suggestion that we abandon our current mythology altogether, but merely to propose that our modern outlook is particularly adapted to framing our sense of who we are, as individuals and as a society, in a way that does not include the wholeness of our totality.

Splitting our perception in this way comes at a cost, highlighting our separate and individual natures, whilst making it more difficult to see and appreciate our dependency, interconnectedness, and wholeness. The current crises that our world faces are, in part, reflections of this blind spot in our outlook. We will explore this in more depth in the next chapter, but first, let us consider wholeness and splitting within our personal psychologies.

The wholeness of "self"

In order to grasp the impact of dividing ourselves, we have to grasp what we are splitting apart from: our wholeness. Jung's concept of the "Self" (with a capital S) is a good place to begin our understanding. Jung viewed the "Self" as a person's whole and total nature.[19] The "Self" is much vaster than simply who we think we are. It is not only our day-to-day personality, but also includes all the subconscious aspects of ourselves that remain hidden and unknown to us: our conscious experience is just the tip of the iceberg. Jung envisioned personal growth as the process of our day-to-day selves becoming ever more aligned with the totality of our greater "Self" and its mysterious wisdom, which is more than just the sum of its parts. Jung came to associate the ancient Indian symbol of the "mandala", meaning "circle" in Sanskrit, with the "Self". Just like circular time, the circular "Self" is not something that can be divided; it is totality itself.

As the "Self" is fundamentally whole, it is impossible to truly cut off from the parts of ourselves that we do not like. When we try to banish a part of ourselves, we end up merely denying it, and whilst it may disappear from our conscious awareness, it nevertheless continues existing in our subconscious minds. We therefore end up not only in conflict with the parts of ourselves we have exiled, but at war with the wholeness of our "Self". Instead of seeing these rejected parts as belonging to us, we view them as if they exist outside of ourselves in order to preserve the illusions of our selective identities. This "projection" leads us into conflict not only with ourselves, but with others too.

Homophobia and projection

When we project out the parts of ourselves that we do not like, we also project out and externalise our inner relationships to them. A good example of this is when fundamentalist hate preachers who are obsessed with condemning the gay community are later understood to have had same-sex relationships themselves. The crusade of hatred to banish homosexuality in the world can be seen as a mirror of the inner violence with which they relate to their own disowned and projected sexuality (which itself is a reflection of a homophobic story that has been internalised from culture).[20] As an experiment, you can ask yourself, "Am I in denial of any aspect of my own sexuality as a result of my prejudices?" As you do so, pay particular attention to the thoughts and feelings that you notice. Do you find yourself wondering openly and curiously about this, or do you notice a resistance that shuts down the process of spending time with this question? If so, it is worth wondering whether this may reflect either an aversion to acknowledging an aspect of your sexuality or an unwillingness to see yourself as someone who may be holding a prejudice or judgement.

Noticing inner resistance to how we want to see ourselves gives us clues as to where we might be denying parts of ourselves that we do not want to accept. When we cannot be open to the possibility of identifying with something, there is a good chance we are relating to it through the lens of projection, seeing it as something that belongs exclusively to others. This, however, precludes the possibility of having an inner relationship to it and therefore of integrating it into a bigger and more whole self. It is through the process of relationship, both inner and outer, that we ultimately grow. Returning to our previous question, this could mean either coming to a greater connection to and acceptance of our own sexuality or to a growing awareness and acknowledgement of our prejudices. Being open to seeing ourselves in ways we do not like is difficult, as it requires us to question our own identity. However, where we are able to open up to ourselves in this vulnerable way, we have the opportunity to develop a conscious relationship to previously denied aspects of ourselves. When we can bear the discomfort of seeing ourselves as holding prejudices, we are able to consciously change the outdated maps and templates that we may have inherited. Furthermore, by opening up to previously denied aspects of ourselves, such as facets of our sexuality or emotions we once deemed unacceptable, we can allow these parts to enrich our lives with their vitality and the new possibilities for connection they present, allowing us to more fully embody our greater "Self".

Edward

Our dependent needs, being so often disowned, are prime candidates for projection. When we deny our vulnerability, we end up projecting it out onto the world, seeing it in others through the filter of our negative judgements. This process featured heavily in a variety of different ways in my work with Edward.

Edward was a middle-aged man who came to therapy to help cope with "stress". Upon first meeting Edward, I was struck by his loud voice and an air of self-assurance. However, as he sat down and began talking, I realised that despite my initial impression of confidence, there was a vulnerable sensitivity that lay just below the surface that I immediately warmed to. Edward worked in finance, had been married for fifteen years, and had a three-year-old boy called Jack. At first, Edward was quite vague about what he meant by "stress", but over time he began to open up about the difficulties he was experiencing as a new father. Whilst he loved his son, Edward described how he had difficulty connecting with him and had been struggling with feelings of depression, frustration, guilt, and anger. After a particularly intense outburst of anger, Edward had been encouraged by his wife to seek help. The exchange below happened a few months after we had started therapy.

Client—Edward (E) and Therapist—Joseph (J)

E: I spend all day at work, and when I come home, she's with Jack. I try to do my bit, of course … it's difficult, you know.

J: Like you do your bit …

E: Yeah … I do my bit, but it feels like there's nothing in it for me.

J: Like you don't receive anything back?

E: Well, yes … like I'm on the outside.

J: On the outside looking in?

E: Yeah … like there's this invisible barrier between them and me. (*Edward has gone still.*)

J: What do you see when you look in?

E: The way he is the centre of her world and … she's so caring … it's what I want … (*His eyes well up with tears.*)

In being faced with his son, a helpless newborn baby, Edward was forced to face his relationship to his own dependency and vulnerability. Growing up, Edward had learnt that his need to be looked after by others would not only go unfulfilled, but would be actively shamed and humiliated. As a result, Edward had numbed himself and disconnected from his own feelings of helplessness, vulnerability, and need. He now found the numb and disconnected relationship that he had with his vulnerability, externalised and projected onto his son: it sat between them like an invisible wall. This exchange in therapy marked a significant moment for Edward as he was able to connect with and embody his own need to be cared for. Edward would later describe how, from this point onwards, he found himself increasingly feeling more connected to the warmth that he felt for his son. In being able to form a relationship with his own dependent and vulnerable self, the invisible veil between him and his son lifted. This can be understood as the withdrawal of a projection: in becoming conscious of the vulnerability in himself, Edward was now able to see and connect to the external reality of his son, rather than simply seeing his own externalised, disowned vulnerability. This also brought about a broader softening in the way that Edward related to vulnerability in general, in both himself and others.

In the following months, Edward began to recount his experience of going to a traditional and prestigious boarding school. "Going to", however, falls short of conveying his experience, which, in his words, felt more akin to being "forced" and "cast out". The sense of abandonment and rejection he felt from his parents deeply impacted him (a feeling he re-experienced when he felt left out after the birth of his son). Before he could process this abrupt disconnection from his parents, he found himself having to deal with the harsh environment of boarding school, where he had to survive on his own. To make matters worse, when he arrived, he soon discovered that any show of vulnerability would be quickly preyed on with humiliating ridicule from the other boys. Edward found himself with a cruel nickname for the rest of his time there. He was not alone in his torment; everyone received a fair share of bullying along with a nickname that was often based on a critical incident in which their vulnerability was exposed. This was not an environment where he could face or recover from his feelings of abandonment.

Looking at Edward's boarding school experience, a complex web of projected vulnerability is revealed. Many parents who send their children to this particular type of boarding school have themselves been through the same experience and therefore learnt that dependency is a weakness that they are better off without. With this in mind, they enrol their children in boarding school in order to best prepare them for the harsh reality of a world where vulnerability is not accepted. In order to survive, the students disconnect from their own "weaknesses" and project them onto others, attacking any "blubbering" that might threaten to remind them of their own tears. This forms the basis of a culture of bullying, which, in addition to targeting vulnerability, takes aim at any incompetency, inferiority, and weakness.

It is easy to imagine how many of the students who attend a prestigious boarding school like Edward's go on to form an identity based on strength, self-sufficiency, and superiority. Often this identity goes hand-in-hand with an internalised sense of class. The corresponding qualities of weakness, dependency, and inferiority are disowned and need to be located elsewhere. Unfortunately, these qualities often end up being projected onto the "lower class", along with the accompanying attitude of contempt that they have experienced first-hand towards their own vulnerability. Richard Beard in *Sad Little Men* describes how some boarding schools systematically take aim at vulnerability and weakness in order to prepare their students for the challenges of running "the Empire".[21] This perpetuates the narratives that contribute towards justifying the injustice of colonialism, as we have already explored in Chapter 2. Whilst the number of people who attend such schools is very small, the narratives that are found there are particularly significant, as an incredibly high proportion of Britain's politicians have attended similar schools and therefore these stories come to underpin much of our culture and the way we structure our society.

Whilst it may be easy to judge this "elite" segment of society, to do so would be to project our own capacity to disown our vulnerability onto it, turning the attention away from the ways in which we may also deny our dependency. To get carried away with blame would be to fall under the spell of the same narrative that is taught at boarding school: that the "upper class" are not themselves vulnerable. This vulnerability is not reflected in material wealth, of course, but rather in emotional wounding and the way in which they are embedded in stories that make it very hard for their psychological needs to be met or to experience a greater connection to the world. This endless web of projected vulnerability not only exists in boarding schools such as Edward's, but can be found in every part of society. This includes some of the least privileged communities in our society, where adverse life experiences can contribute to the message that vulnerability is not welcome. Seeing the "bad" as being located in only one part of our society, wherever that may be, is to see the world through a split perspective.

Hate

Hate splits us apart. It is the fuel that fires projection and "othering". When we hate something, we define ourselves against it, pushing it away so that it appears to us as a distant other. When we locate the "bad" outside ourselves, we split off from the wholeness of our "Self", creating division both within ourselves and with others. Whilst our hatred appears to be a very outwards-facing energy, it often conceals a hidden internal war. For every part of the world we hate has an inner counterpart: an aspect of ourselves that we are trying to escape. It is an interesting exercise to reflect on someone or something that you hate. As you contemplate the object of your hatred, try to recognise and define the qualities that you particularly do not like. Once you have identified these, reflect on your relationship to these qualities. Is there an aspect of yourself that you are struggling to accept?

Whenever there is a strong rejection or hatred of something, it is likely that there is a process of splitting happening close by. As a therapist, it is valuable to keep this in mind when a client speaks of someone or something they hate. When this happens, it is useful to have one ear listening to them as if they are really speaking about an aspect of themselves. It is worth bearing in mind that the projected aspects of ourselves are subconscious and, by their very nature, the parts of ourselves that we least want to identify with. As a result of this, confronting a client with an interpretation that attempts to join them prematurely with the object of their hatred rarely goes down well. However, by resisting the urge to meet a client head-on with our analysis and instead simply holding the possibility of their projection in mind, a client can come to rediscover organically the disowned aspect of themselves at their own pace. Uncovering and accepting the parts of ourselves that we would rather not acknowledge is the process of reclaiming our projections and finding new integrated inner relationships to them. In doing so, we not only expand our sense of self so that it more closely resembles the totality of our "Self", but we also open up the possibility of connecting to the world directly and not through the filter of our projections, as Edward did with his son.

Stories that polarise

The stories we tell each other, particularly those that become foundational to our identity, influence how easily we are able to connect with the wholeness of our inner being and the diversity of our outer worlds. The narratives that make up our sense of self, of who we think we are, mark the boundaries of where we see ourselves ending and the world beginning. When we do not feel safe, we may look for narratives that promise us reassurance with their fortified boundaries and solid definitions of "self" and "other". So often, the same "us and them" stories that attempt to provide us with safety within the confines of their well-defined identities also appeal to us by placing all of the qualities that we do not like in the camp of "them": as projections. However, we cannot fully separate from either the wholeness of our "Self" or the totality of the world. Our projections will therefore continue to haunt us, threatening us by simply existing. The walls we initially put up to protect ourselves become the very things that define and create the enemy we feel we need to defend against. In fact, it is not only our rigid identities that polarise us, but any narrative that we relate to as a concrete and literal truth will, by virtue of its fixed and solid nature, cast a shadow of denial that creates division. In order to bring down these walls and connect more deeply with ourselves and others, we must become aware at ever-increasing depths of the stories and identities that we have taken as truths, softening our relationship to them as we go.

Just as hatred can reveal an opportunity for greater connection to the wholeness of the "Self" when we become aware of its projections, so too can "otherness". When we open up to the "other" that we define our sense of self against, our narrow conceptions of self are expanded in the process. Whilst it is easier to be understanding of those who view the world in the same way as we do, it is much more difficult to understand and connect to somebody who sees the world from a vastly different perspective. In order to truly empathise and connect with others who are very different to us, we need to be able to see the world through their eyes. To do so, we must become vulnerable and let go, for a moment, of the stories that keep us safe, making space in our being for otherness to enter. It is this vulnerable opening that has the gentle power to soften the hatred that closes us off from the world and from our deeper selves.

Summary

In the modern Western paradigm, we view the world through the lens of stories that emphasise our independent existence at the expense of making it more difficult to be in touch with the wholeness of our "Self". When we reject and banish the parts of ourselves that we do not like, such as our vulnerability and dependency, we split the wholeness of our "Self" into parts. We incorporate the "good parts" into our identities and project the parts that we do not like out onto the world, judging them as though they really belong to others. When this process gathers momentum, we end up embroiled in hatred, which divides us in the most profound ways. In order to find a deeper connection with our inner being and outer world, we must dare to be vulnerable, opening ourselves up to otherness by releasing our grip on the stories that define our sense of self.

CHAPTER 7

The denial of interdependency

According to Buddhist philosophy, dependency is not only an aspect of our human relationships, but the very basis of reality itself. From this perspective, existence is an indivisible whole that is made up of interdependency itself. When we contemplate this deeply, we can understand how the narratives of our separate and independent identities are illusory constructs. By examining Buddhist ideas, this chapter explores what happens when we split off, not only from our "Self", but from the totality of our interdependency. In so doing, we uncover the denial that lies at the very heart of both the climate crisis and our modern alienation from the world.

Interdependence

> It really boils down to this: that all life is interrelated. We are all caught in an inescapable network of mutuality, tied into a single garment of destiny. Whatever affects one directly, affects all indirectly. We are made to live together because of the interrelated structure of reality. Did you ever stop to think that you can't leave for your job in the morning without being dependent on most of the world? You get up in the morning and go to the bathroom and reach over for the sponge, and that's handed to you by a Pacific

> islander. You reach for a bar of soap, and that's given to you at the hands of a Frenchman. And then you go into the kitchen to drink your coffee for the morning, and that's poured into your cup by a South American. And maybe you want tea: that's poured into your cup by a Chinese. Or maybe you're desirous of having cocoa for breakfast, and that's poured into your cup by a West African. And then you reach over for your toast, and that's given to you at the hands of an English-speaking farmer, not to mention the baker. And before you finish eating breakfast in the morning, you've depended on more than half of the world. This is the way our universe is structured, this is its interrelated quality. We aren't going to have peace on earth until we recognize this basic fact of the interrelated structure of all reality. (Martin Luther King)[22]

The interrelated quality that Martin Luther King is referring to here can be described as interdependence. Interdependence is the way in which all things in some way rely on and connect to each other. In Buddhist philosophy, interdependence is the very fabric of reality. This is a concept known as "*Pratītyasamutpāda*" in Sanskrit, translated as "dependent origination" or "independent co-arising".[23] Dependent origination describes both the interconnected nature of reality and the chain of causative factors that leads to suffering. We will come back to these causative factors later, but for now, we will explore the interconnected nature of dependent origination. Dependent origination means that every little thing that exists is not only connected to, but is totally inseparable from, everything else in the universe.

> If we look into this sheet of paper even more deeply, we can see the sunshine in it. If the sunshine is not there, the forest cannot grow. In fact, nothing can grow. Even we cannot grow without sunshine. And so, we know that the sunshine is also in this sheet of paper. The paper and the sunshine inter-are. And if we continue to look, we can see the logger who cut the tree and brought it to the mill to be transformed into paper. And we see the wheat. We know the logger cannot exist without his daily bread, and therefore the wheat that became his bread is also in this sheet of paper. And the logger's father and mother are in it too. When we look in this way, we see that without all of these things, this sheet of paper cannot exist. Looking even more deeply, we can see we are in it too. This is not

> difficult to see, because when we look at a sheet of paper, the sheet of paper is part of our perception. Your mind is in here, and mine is also. So we can say that everything is in here with this sheet of paper. You cannot point out one thing that is not here-time, space, the earth, the rain, the minerals in the soil, the sunshine, the cloud, the river, the heat. Everything co-exists with this sheet of paper. That is why I think the word inter-be should be in the dictionary. "To be" is to inter-be. You cannot just be by yourself alone. You have to inter-be with every other thing. This sheet of paper is, because everything else is. (Thich Nhat Hanh)[24]

This is a beautiful description of the ever-present wholeness of dependent origination. It is also a gentle challenge to our perception of a separate and independent self. Just as the developmental psychologist Winnicott said that there is "*no such thing as an infant*",[25] due to its existence being fundamentally dependent on its caregiver, there is also no such thing as a self (that exists outside of its relationship to all things). Dependent origination implies not only that we exist in relationship to all things, but that all things exist *only* by virtue of their relationship to each other. Hot only exists in relation to cold, good to bad, left to right and high to low: nothing has any intrinsic reality or real basis in and of itself. This lack of independent reality to any one thing is what is known as the concept of "*śūnyatā*" in Sanskrit, translated as "emptiness". This carries huge implications for the reality of the self, which, from a Buddhist perspective, lacks any real substance, which is to say there is no independent reality nor underlying, unchanging foundation to the self. This is known as the concept of "*anattā*" or "no-self". As our sense of self strives to create a feeling of safety through the illusion of its continuity, solidity, and control, the reality of dependent origination can feel deeply threatening to us. As a result, we tend to deny our interconnectedness and instead seek refuge in our illusions of separateness. As we will see, it is this flawed coping strategy that is at the root of our suffering.

Whilst these Buddhist concepts can be difficult to understand, it is worth keeping in mind that much of Buddhist philosophy is focused on our personal experience of reality, rather than in creating an objective map to follow. These ideas are only as valuable to the extent that we can relate them to our own experience. The real essence of Buddhism is to investigate the nature of our self first hand: to look and see for ourselves.

The fiction of the self

The map is not the territory.
—Alfred Korzybski[26]

The most important story we tell ourselves is the story of our self: our ego. It is so fundamental to how we see the world that it is hard to appreciate it as being a work of fiction. Let us return to the metaphor from the first chapter of the pair of glasses that we use to see the world. The lenses of these glasses are made up of the stories, templates, and maps that we develop as we grow up and through which we end up subconsciously viewing the world. We are so at home wearing the spectacles of the self, were we to go swimming, we would undoubtedly jump in the pool with them still on. The self can seem like the most "self-evident" truth that there is. However, is there something we overlook about its nature by its very virtue of being so fundamental to our perception? In fact, what is the self? Can you point to it? Is it real? It is common to feel quite outraged when first confronted with the notion that the self may not exist. After all, if these stories are the clothes within which we seek psychological shelter, being asked to discard our self is equivalent to being asked to strip totally naked!

If we take the Buddhist idea of "no-self" to be true, our sense of self and therefore our sense of psychological safety, continuity, and meaning, are called into question. To perceive our entangled interdependency is to see how everything exists only in relationship to everything else. It is to see that we have no inside nor outside, no beginning nor end, no fixed nor enduring centre: no real self. This can feel equivalent to facing annihilation. Because the psychological clothing of the self is not objectively real, we are always going to feel exposed and vulnerable. However, in order to try and find some vestige of certainty and continuity, we tend to cling to our stories and identities, hoping that they can provide us with something solid to hang on to. However, no story can ever provide for us the enduring certainty that we long for. The more we try to make our stories definitive, permanent, and absolute, the more that the changing and subjective nature of reality will seem to threaten them and therefore threaten us. The solution to this downward spiral of existential insecurity is to do the very thing we fear: to let go and surrender to the powerlessness of our interdependency. However, before we follow this path to deeper interconnection, we must descend a little further into our fears and illusions.

Mother Earth

Our fears of interdependency and dependency are inseparably linked. Dependency not only triggers our terrifying memories of the "weather-scapes" of early life, but also faces us with our interdependency and the existential threat that this poses to our sense of self. Likewise, connecting with our interdependent nature touches on our fears of dependency and all they entail. Our deepest fears, of depending on others and of losing our sense of self, are deeply entwined. Reminders of our dependency and interdependency surround us everywhere we go, and therefore we inevitably end up having to seek shelter in denial. Nowhere can this be more clearly seen than in our relationship to the living environment and the climate crisis we now face.

We exist in a state of total and utter dependence on the environment that surrounds us. We count on it in every moment to sustain us. With every breath we take, we take for granted the very air we need to continue living. Anybody who has been underwater or without breath for too long is immediately aware of this vulnerability. It would be too overwhelming to be aware of the gravity of this dependence in every moment. So instead, we go about our lives taking the sustenance we find around us for granted and ignoring the vulnerability of always being at the mercy of an otherness much greater than us. In this way, our relationship to the environment is much like a baby's very early experience of their mother: a fact that is reflected in cultures all over the world by the many different names they refer to "Mother Earth": Pachamama, Terra, Gaia, and Prithvi, amongst many others.

For most of our time on Earth, our dependence on nature for survival has never been in question. The sun, moon, ocean, and stars were acknowledged as the forces on which life depends. Nature was feared, praised, appeased, and respected. It was the home of the Gods, and we humbly submitted to the power of their forces. As human civilisation has developed, our ability to provide for ourselves as a species has increased dramatically. Developments in science and technology have meant that we are increasingly self-reliant, and many of us no longer live in such a state of vulnerable exposure. In our dry, warm houses that are illuminated without the need for the sun, it is easy to fall for the illusion that we are independent from the world outside. However, we are now becoming witnesses to the destruction of our natural environment and are beginning to feel the impact that its collapse might have on us. Climate change and a future of climate catastrophe threatens to confront us once again with our dependency on Mother Earth for our survival.

Reckoning with the reality of an impending climate collapse, the templates and memories of what it means to be dependent are awakened from their subconscious slumber. Both the "weatherscapes" of our early experiences and our vision of climate collapse trigger catastrophic scenes of what happens when the sustaining environment that we depend on lets us down: huge storms, being flooded, hungry, thirsty, too hot or too cold. The climate crisis faces us with powerlessness, helplessness, and dependency that mirror the most primal and evocative early memories that we have been running from. Naturally, we seek shelter.

Self-sufficiency

In the same manner in which we deny our dependency in our interpersonal relationships, we deny our need for the Earth and foster the illusion of our separateness and self-sufficiency. In this respect, our own psychological development from babies to adults mirrors the development of civilisation. Just as we were once exposed and dependent on the sustaining presence of our primary caregiver, our prehistoric selves were more vulnerable to the moods of nature and possessed far less control over the regulation of their environment. Growing "up", historically and developmentally, has meant that we have developed a greater capacity to look after ourselves. We are more able to meet our own physical needs, regulate our own emotions, and cope with aloneness. As a species, we have developed technologies, such as shelter, farming techniques, and means of harvesting energy, which means we are able to provide an increasingly safe and stable environment for ourselves. As adults and as an "adult" civilisation, we are able to be self-sufficient … to an extent.

Our modern civilisation embraces our independence from nature with gusto. In fact, the society we live in today could be described as having an avoidant attachment style: hoping to find security and regulation in itself rather than in a relationship with another. Just as in an avoidant attachment style, our need for otherness is denied, with modern technology affording us the fantasy that we can be capable enough to be truly self-sufficient. Our relationship to the environment has taken this principle to the extreme. The more technology has developed, allowing our society to feel insulated from its dependency on nature, the more society has operated as if it really were self-sufficient. It is the denial of our dependency, our illusion of self-sufficiency, that is polluting our world. It is not a coincidence that many of the technologies that enable our "self-sufficient" fantasy lead to the destruction of the environment.

There is a remarkable parallel to the process of interpersonal self-sabotage here. Because our society fears the precariousness of its dependency, it attacks the source of its care: the sustaining environment itself. In our personal relationships, attacking the other person serves to cut us off from our disturbing feelings of dependency by attempting to destroy the relationship that is triggering these feelings. We are doing the same thing, as a species, with the environment: lashing out at the Earth that sustains us in order to avoid confronting the fragile position that we are really in. This can be imagined as either an active act of self-sabotage or a passive process of denial. For when we deny our need for another and ignore the connection that exists between us, we often impact and hurt who (or what) we are depending on, creating an even more vulnerable state of relationship. The hurt and damage that we create becomes evidence of our connection and dependency: a reflection of our true state of need, and so that too is denied. The more we hide from our dependency on the Earth, the more we damage it, creating more vulnerability and further fuelling our denial. It is a vicious cycle.

In addition to attacking the other, self-sabotaging involves denying and cutting off from the part of ourselves that longs for connection: the part of us that has a deep need that might be met and satiated. In hiding from our vulnerable need for the Earth, we are cutting off from our capacity to relate to nature from a place of depth, longing, imagination and vitality. Reconnecting with our environment also means reconnecting with this part of ourselves. Behind our climate crisis lies a profound opportunity to discover a depth that we have long been ignoring as a culture. We will explore this potential in Chapter 10. First, however, there are more layers of denial to peel back.

Our separate nature

Denial, as we know, carries out its work through the telling of stories. We weave narratives that exclude our own feelings of vulnerable dependency and make alternative explanations for our experience. These stories, however, have repercussions of their own, often deepening divisions in how we relate to each other and to the world around us.

One such narrative that lies at the heart of our disturbed relationship to the environment is that of our own human supremacy over nature. The natural world around us is seen as valuable only in terms of what it can provide for us, not in and of itself. We do not view it as an equal other that might possess agency, intelligence, feeling, or soul. The more that we perceive ourselves as separate and superior to the natural world, the more we labour under the illusion that we can take from the environment for our own separate gain. It is the perception of separateness that is both the cause and result of our increasingly exploitative relationship to nature. We tell ourselves that nature, our victim, is without value. This story justifies our actions and creates a further perception of division from our natural world. Despite our justifications, beneath the story of our supremacy lies a profound collective shame for our actions. In order to acknowledge that we are surrounded by a living other, we have to confront our treatment of it. Facing this shame becomes a barrier to our connection to nature that we cannot bring ourselves to bear. Instead, we fall back into our stories of denial, vindicating our actions and affirming our separateness. In the same way, the self tells a narrative of its independent, continuous existence. Similarly, we, the human race, tell a story of denial: that we are truly separate from the rest of nature. In doing so, we hope to avoid both our dependency and the pain of our wounded relationship to the Earth.

Our story of supremacy endows only our human race with meaningful worth and soul. The consequence of this is that the rest of the world is starved of depth, meaning, and significance. Instead, we view the world as if it were fundamentally dead, and we live with apathy, numbness, sadness, and depression as a result. In order to imagine a world beyond the limitations of our modern story, it is first necessary to face our shame and feel the pain that is being covered up and denied by our narratives of separation and supremacy. The suffering that this disconnection causes does not belong to us alone: we share it with the Earth. It is in this wound, therefore, that our union with nature is concealed. The guilt, shame, fear, and grief we feel in relation to our wounded environment are gateways to deeper connection when we can brave facing them.

The Garden of Eden

> When the woman saw that the fruit of the tree was good for food and pleasing to the eye, and also desirable for gaining wisdom, she took some and ate it. She also gave some to her husband, who was with her, and he ate it. Then the eyes of both of them were opened, and they realized they were naked; so they sewed fig leaves together and made coverings for themselves.[27]

In this modern age, as we witness the destruction of the natural world around us, it is easy to imagine that humanity has fallen from the Garden of Eden. Where we were once in union with Mother Earth, we now stand naked, ashamed, and separate. In a way, we also make this journey through the course of our psychological development: from the timeless oneness of early life to the isolation and exposure that our self-consciousness brings. As we grow and develop, the maps and narratives we construct solidify our sense of self and therefore deepen our sense of separation from the world, much like the fruit from the tree of knowledge did for Adam and Eve. The more we "know" the world, the more we close off to our immediate experience of it and become separated from others with our certainty.

The fall from the Garden of Eden not only depicts our journey into separateness as a species and over the course of our personal development, but also describes the arc of our moment-to-moment becoming: the chain of causations of "dependent origination". In addition to referring to our interdependency, "dependent origination" describes the process by which we "fall" from eternal nirvana into the time-bound dualistic world of life and death, suffering as a result. The first link in this chain is described as "ignorance": our failure to perceive our infinite and eternal interdependency. Instead of seeing the world as it really is, we see it through the filters of our maps and templates, which obscure and diminish our perception of our whole nature. This is to see life through the lens of the narratives that make up the clothing of the self: to be in denial of our interconnectedness. From this divided viewpoint, we see things in terms of "black" and "white"; "self", and "other"; "good" and "bad". When we see the world from this split perspective, we grasp after it, striving after the good and avoiding the bad. It is this push and pull, our rejection of the way things are, that leads to our suffering. Therefore, whilst denial tempts us with its stories of independent selfhood that promise security, ultimately, the divided perception it leaves us with is the root cause of our pain. According to Buddhist philosophy, to alleviate suffering we must reverse this chain by accepting things as they are, thereby seeing through the illusions of our stories of separation and perceiving our interdependent origination. Or to put it more succinctly, in the words of Zen Master Seung Sahn: "Only don't know."[28]

To perceive our interdependency is to connect with absolutely everything: the rich diversity of our inner being and outer world. It is to connect to wholeness itself. However, connecting with the oneness of everything is not always the ecstatic experience that we might imagine it to be. Our wholeness contains within it both the good and the bad, not just the selective truth that the stories of our cultures and sense of self present us with. We are confronted with the parts of ourselves and our realities that lie beyond our denial: the personal and collective wounds that we seek to become separate from. However, whilst it may bring us pain, it is through facing our wounds and embracing our abandoned vulnerabilities that we can reconnect with the wholeness of our interdependency—a process we explore in the following chapters.

Summary

Reality is a web of interconnected dependency: our "dependent origination". All things exist only insofar as they relate to everything else; nothing exists independently, including ourselves. Our dependency and interdependency therefore pose a threat to the existential foundations that our sense of self is built on, and as a result, we deny them. This is evident in our relationship with the environment, where we deny our dependence on it to preserve the illusion of independent control and security. Ultimately, however, the denial of our interdependency leads to our suffering, causing us to hurt each other and to "fall" out of eternal wholeness into our experience of a separate self in a time-bound, dualistic world. The key to alleviating our suffering is therefore to loosen our grip on the stories of separation that denial tells us and instead, embrace the world and ourselves as they really are.

CHAPTER 8

The return of the exiled

The key to reconnecting with our greater wholeness lies in our abandoned vulnerabilities. These tender parts of our being, however, are hidden behind walls we built to protect ourselves. Though cut off, these forgotten parts long to break free and receive the care they so deeply yearn for. Breaking through, however, can often feel like breaking down, as it is our symptoms that mark the reawakening of our suppressed vulnerability, guiding us to seek the help we need. To begin this exploration of how our exiled vulnerability finds its way back to life, we will start by examining narcissism and uncovering the hidden vulnerabilities, longings, and unmet needs that lie beneath its protective shell.

The longing of Narcissus

Narcissism has captured the imagination of our modern culture. We are fascinated by the idea of someone who is obsessively preoccupied with themselves. Perhaps, in narcissists, we see a reflection of ourselves: a state of being and a way of seeing the world that we are all, on some level, familiar with. There is certainly something about narcissism that speaks to our modern age of self-obsession, with each of us transfixed on our screens, grooming the persona we display to the world and eagerly awaiting the arrival of "likes". Narcissism is something that we find great satisfaction in spotting in the world around us, but would not want to identify with ourselves. In this sense, it is often a projected and exiled aspect of ourselves: a part of us that is misunderstood and even demonised. In returning to the original myth of Narcissus, perhaps we can find some understanding that can rekindle our compassion for this misunderstood corner of our psyches.

> Narcissus was a beautiful, enigmatic young man. Many desired him, including the woodland nymph Echo. But Narcissus spurned all affections, including Echo's, such was the extent of his pride. Echo, who was cursed to only repeat back another's words, was devastated. Upon seeing her upset, the other nymphs persuaded Nemesis to curse Narcissus with the same unbearable pain of unrequited love that Echo had experienced. Narcissus, having been cursed, caught sight of his own reflection in a pool of clear water and was set ablaze with love. But try as he might, he could not reach his beloved. He became trapped in a wretched state of longing: grasping after a love that could never be fulfilled. Eventually, after many years, he wasted away and died, still yearning after his reflection. Where his body lay to rest, a yellow flower grew.[29]

Narcissus is a figure of intense longing, of love that wants to make contact with another, but suffers the tragic fate of being cursed to a circular and unfulfilled existence. It is this longing that is the key to understanding narcissism. Whilst a narcissist may appear as if they are only in love with themselves, they secretly long for another. This longing, however, is hidden beneath a grandiose exterior—an identity of superiority that denies vulnerability and conceals a deeply fragile sense of self beneath. Like a delicate seedling, this frail self is sheltered from exposure to the harsh elements of the outer world by the hard shell of its polished surface persona. This whole process happens almost entirely outside of a narcissist's conscious awareness. They really believe their own facade, and it is easy for an onlooker to do the same. This, however, is a tragic misunderstanding. Whilst it may seem like they are in love with the mirror, it is "mirroring" that they truly long for.

Mirroring

As infants, our sense of self is developed in relationship to others. One of our most important psychological needs as we develop is to be "mirrored". To be mirrored is to see ourselves reflected back to us in the eyes of an appreciative other.[30] It is through the "mirror" of the other person that we come to know what we are feeling and who we are, helping us to connect the feelings of our inner world to our sense of self. Furthermore, when the image we see reflected back to us is accompanied by a look of sparkling admiration, we come to feel worthy and wanted. This is a need that we continue to have throughout our lives. For example, when we tell a friend about a difficult experience that we have had, we are seeking both their understanding and approval. When our friend reflects back to us an accurate recognition of what we have gone through, along with a sense of validation and warm acceptance, we leave the interaction understanding and valuing ourselves more than we did at the start. Mirroring is an essential ingredient to our growth, just as warmth, light, and water are to seedlings. This is the mirror that a narcissist truly longs for. The tragedy of narcissism, however, is that the self that they present to the mirror is only a mask. Therefore, the reflection that they receive back does not help them to affirm the worth or reality of the hidden self beneath: the sustenance of mirroring cannot get through the outer shell and nourish the seedling beneath.

Our modern culture is caught in a similar narcissistic fate. The vulnerability of our hunger to connect with each other is buffered by the masks that we put on to display to the world. Nowhere is this more apparent than in the world of social media. On social media, we present a carefully crafted version of ourselves to the world. We sculpt and manicure our masks so that we can receive admiration and validation. However, the stories we tell about ourselves are far from authentic, and so any validation we do receive leaves us feeling empty and unsatisfied.

Social media is also a good reminder of why we wear masks and seek protection in the first place. The anonymity and distance of online interaction can bring out the worst in us. We can act out our hatred and spite, taking aim at others as if they were not real people. We are shielded from each other's humanity and so end up treating each other inhumanely. Social media is not somewhere that is a safe place to expose our vulnerability indiscriminately. In the "Wild West" of the online world, our masks and avatars are the armour we need to survive. The modern world gives us plenty of options to connect from behind our defensive strongholds. For example, communicating via text gives us time to think of our replies, leaving us less exposed and vulnerable, but also making it harder to make real contact as our communications are reduced to a less immediate form. Whilst we may long to connect with others, when we hide behind the shield of our screens, we cut ourselves off from the possibility of deeper connection.

Whilst our technology can lead us to fortify our defences against vulnerability and dependency, it also holds the potential to connect us. The internet, for example, is at its core a giant network made only of interconnectedness itself, not unlike the structure of "dependent origination". Despite its problems, it clearly offers us unparalleled possibilities for connection, the likes of which we have not seen before. In understanding the interplay between feeling protected and being vulnerable, perhaps we can harness our technology in a way that builds broader and deeper connections, rather than causing further entrenchment in our defences. As with all possibilities for connection, there is a tension between exposure and safety. In opening up, we risk subjecting ourselves to the storms and harsh weather that can shake our seedlings to the core. However, in revealing ourselves more profoundly, we can be mirrored as who we truly are and receive the nourishment we need to grow.

Tragic misunderstandings

It is a tragedy when the stories that we tell the world to keep our vulnerability hidden are wholeheartedly believed. We long to be found, but dare not risk revealing ourselves. This is a difficult dilemma. Likewise, when we take someone else at face value and fail to see beneath their armour, we tragically lose sight of their vulnerability and therefore their humanity too. In the case of narcissism, when we cannot see the frailty of the person behind the mask, all we see is a grotesque "Wizard of Oz" figure, whom we dehumanise because we mistakenly think they are all-powerful. When we refer to someone as a "narcissist", we reduce the spectrum of their full being to a one-dimensional aspect. This is not to say that we should relate without caution to those with a mask on, as there is indeed great potential for hurt. However, we should not view narcissists with malice either, as to do so would be to fall for the illusion of the grandiose invulnerability that is being portrayed. Rather, we should try to relate to "narcissists" with understanding and compassion, so that we are able to see beneath their defensive exteriors and glimpse their hidden frailty below. Just as in the *Wizard of Oz*, when we see through the illusion of the great wizard, we are able to find power in ourselves, rather than waiting for it to be given to us by another person. In this way, seeing the vulnerability of others can keep us from falling into the illusions of their defence mechanisms and getting hurt as a result.

Misunderstandings bring about a unique and silent pain. To be seen in a way that that feels untrue or negative, feels like an attack on our very selves. Whilst being mirrored helps to strengthen our sense of self, being misunderstood does the opposite, creating dissonance, confusion, and leaving us feeling as though we are bad or unworthy in some way. However, misunderstandings are unavoidable. As we grow up, one of the most detrimental ways we can be misunderstood is if our attempts to have our needs met are misinterpreted. For example, when our sense of self is feeling fragile and in need of support, we might seek out some affirmation. If we do not find the mirroring we need, we escalate our attempts to be seen. When our cries go unanswered, we find ourselves having to shout louder. It is easy to see how these attempts to be praised can be misread and labelled incorrectly as arrogance, misbehaviour, or being a show-off. As a result, it may feel as if we are being told that our need for mirroring is in some way bad or wrong. In being misunderstood, our developmental needs can get misconstrued, and a distorted story may be told about who we are. Sadly, we often internalise these stories and labels and, in doing so, inadvertently deny and exile the vulnerability of our own needs.

Misunderstandings of this nature occur not only during our development but also in our daily lives. If we consider, for a moment, all the judgements that we make about others during our day-to-day lives, perhaps we too are regularly misconstruing the nature of their behaviour. For example, when we are driving and somebody cuts us off, we might view this other person as stupid, selfish, and malicious. However, it might be that this person is running late for a job interview that they desperately need to support their family. Or perhaps this person grew up being bullied, learning from hard experience that if you yield to others, you open yourself up as a target. There is a reason and a meaning behind the difficult and "ill-natured" parts of this world. In understanding these reasons, we unmask the vulnerability of others and naturally feel compassion. By halting our judgements and instead, trying to understand others as though there must be some justifiable need that they are trying to meet (even if we may not feel their actions are justified), we can transform our perception of evil to an understanding that, in the words of Marianne Williamson, "Everything is either love or a call to love."[31]

Resistance

Psychotherapy is not immune to misunderstandings. A popular concept within psychotherapy is the term "resistance". Resistance was, like so many other ideas in psychotherapy, one that was first coined and explored by Freud.[32] Resistance is the idea that the client may sometimes appear to oppose the therapy in order to avoid the pain of confronting their issues. This idea has remained a popular concept in psychotherapy discourse, but is often misused in practice as a catch-all to explain any behaviour from a client that a therapist does not like or runs counter to the therapist's agenda. The client's attempts to have their needs met are often misunderstood as "resistance" and characterised as malevolent and interfering forces.

Looking back to my work with Michael in Chapter 5 demonstrates the way in which a therapist can misunderstand a client and, in doing so, misconstrue their most essential needs. During the early stages of my therapy with Michael, I was under the impression that he would always disagree with me. It seemed as though he was resisting my attempts to understand what he was feeling. However, in interpreting his responses as "resistance", I was misunderstanding him at an essential level. Instead of seeing somebody who was vulnerable, whose experience had taught him that it was not safe to express his need for others, I saw a confident and competitive adult who, somewhat obnoxiously, always wanted to be right. When I viewed him as a competent adult, I felt frustrated and annoyed. However, when I was able to see that this same behaviour stemmed from an underlying vulnerability, I felt a warm compassion towards him instead. These two perspectives hinged on my own inner relationships: when I opened up to my own vulnerability, my feelings of inferiority as a therapist, I was able to see his more clearly.

The more that we are able to recognise and relate sensitively to our own vulnerability, the more we will be able to relate kindly to that of others and vice versa. However, opening up to our vulnerability is something that we cannot do totally on our own: we need the help of others. Yet, if we have buried our unmet needs so deeply that we are totally unaware of them, how do these vulnerabilities ever get unearthed or met? Luckily, the vastness of our subconscious minds, the "Self", has an intelligence that is greater than our conscious minds and, when the conditions are right, will attempt to reunite us with the wounded parts of ourselves that are in exile. Often, this process begins with the appearance of symptoms that we misinterpret as problems to be dispensed with, rather than as opportunities for healing. It is these "problems" that bring my clients to psychotherapy and start them on their journey to connecting with their hidden vulnerability and fuller "Self".

The uninvited guest

Our misunderstood vulnerability is not content with living out its days in the seclusion of its shelter: it longs to break out of its shell and make contact with the outside world, where it can grow and flourish. More often than not, this process resembles a painful and bloody birth that happens seemingly outside of our control. Whilst the process of psychological growth can be messy and confusing, the hidden intelligence of the "Self" is at work behind the scenes.

> This being, my beloved, is a guest house;
> each morning a new visitor arrives.
> Do not feel burdened by their appearance,
> for soon enough they will be gone.
> Whatever comes into your heart from the beyond
> is yours to host, treat them well.
>
> With each moment, a new state enters;
> welcome them all as honoured guests.

Some will bring laughter, some will bring tears,
yet each carries a gift from the invisible world.
If a sorrowful thought darkens your joy,
know that it is preparing the way for joy's return.
It sweeps your house clean of clutter,
so that new gladness can enter from the source of all good.
It shakes the yellow leaves from your heart's branches,
so that fresh green ones can unfurl.
It pulls up the dead twisted root,
revealing the living core below.
Whatever sorrow removes from your heart,
it will restore something greater in its place.

So when a new grief appears at the doorway,
welcome it in like you would an old friend.
(Jalal al-Din Muhammad Rumi)[33]

Symptoms call us on a journey. They break us down, bring us to our knees and push us until we seek help. Whilst many people enter therapy with the hope that their symptoms will vanish, this is often the very opposite of what their "Self" has in mind. Symptoms are not a nuisance to be gotten rid of; they are voices that emerge from the forgotten depths of our being, calling on us to grow. Whilst our symptoms may make us feel hopeless, they are actually the first signs that hope has returned. They mark the beginning of a process of germination: the cracking of the hard shell of our competent personas and the emergence of the tender seedlings of our vulnerability. But before these green shoots can be seen at the surface, we are called to descend into the soil to find and reunite with them in the darkness where we have left them.

In therapy, symptoms are honoured. They are given a voice, welcomed in and listened to with attentive care. Therapy is not the process of trying to change someone or to get them "better". It is a radical acceptance of things as they are. The more that we listen to symptoms, the more coherent their voices become. As we get to know our symptoms better, we may begin to recognise them, not as a foreign invasion, but as the parts of ourselves that we have denied so that we do not have to feel their pain. Rather than push these aspects of our self away, we should draw them closer in a loving embrace. It is often said that it is a paradox that when we accept our difficulties, they finally change. However, when we appreciate that "our difficulties" are living parts of our being, it does not seem paradoxical at all. If we imagine that our symptoms are the voices of the rejected aspects of our being, then we can see how, by accepting them, they cause them to change. Picture a little girl tugging at her mother's leg in distress. "Mummy, Mummy, Mummy ..." she keeps saying, only to be ignored. When her mother finally turns to face her and hears about the difficulties she has been having, it is not a surprise that she no longer needs to keep seeking her mother's attention. However, facing the parts of ourselves that are in distress and hearing their cries is not as easy as it seems and can feel like a descent into the suffering that we had hoped to leave behind.

The walls of trauma

In welcoming back our denied selves, we must face the pain and hurt that we have been hiding from in our denial. We must re-encounter the unfulfilled needs and unacceptable parts of ourselves that were not initially welcomed by others and do not fit in easily with the world around us. We are, once again, presented with the difficulty of finding a way of living alongside the parts of ourselves that are suffering. In facing our difficulties, we are returning to problems that we were unable to solve in the past, and we remember why we chose to forget them in the first place. Therapy, for a while, can feel like we are moving backwards. However, things are not the same when we do not have to face them alone, as we will discover in the next chapter.

To be in exile is to be in a state of trauma. Trauma can be understood as the process of being exposed to a pain or difficulty that is psychologically overwhelming and indigestible. When we are unable to process an experience, when it is too much, too painful or irreconcilable in some way, we cannot weave it into the tapestries of our narratives. Instead, the thread becomes tangled in the loom, creating jumbled meanings that lie outside of our conscious awareness and hinder us. Just as the body will build a wall of tissue around a foreign object to isolate it from the rest of the body, the mind will wall off psychologically indigestible experiences with denial. As we *have* experience, when we wall it off, we are cutting off from a living part of ourselves that is in need and pain. Being cut off is the essence of trauma. What is needed to prevent and heal trauma is connection. When there is another person who is psychologically available to us, our trauma can be digested. This may happen moments after we experience something overwhelming, or years later, when we finally find somebody with whom we can share it. Just like a baby bird needs help digesting their food from their mother, sometimes we need help to digest our experiences.[34] It is this connection that our walled-off trauma longs for: to be untangled and rewoven back into the fabric of life.

Trauma, just like narcissism, is a seed with a hard shell that protects a living part of our being within it. When the conditions are right and hope is stirred, its outer casing breaks and the vulnerability within grows towards the surface. Our exiled selves need us, and we need others. They seek our attention with symptoms, hoping that we may turn towards them once again. They guide us to others by pushing us to seek the help that we need. When we open up to another person with our vulnerability, we can digest and integrate the difficult aspects of life that we have been protecting ourselves from. In doing so, we dissolve the walls that divide us internally and cut us off from others, moving towards the greater wholeness of our "Self" and restoring our connection to the interdependent world that we belong to. This is an organic process with an intelligence that exceeds our conscious awareness. Wholeness is constantly seeking itself; we just need to listen and let its processes unfold.

Wholeness and society

The wounds in our society and culture are not unlike our personal traumas. They represent ruptured and disturbed connections that express collective symptoms, calling for us to attend to them. Just like our personal trauma, walls of denial also exist within our greater collective, locking out our pain and vulnerability. When the narratives that we live by cannot incorporate or include a painful experience, they are written out of our stories with denial, isolating and traumatising the most vulnerable parts of our society. Just as in psychotherapy, bringing down these walls is not a straightforward process.

In order to connect to the aspects of the world that we have collectively cut off from, we must encounter and feel the pain that we have pushed away. Similar to the process of therapy, it can feel as though things get worse before they get better. For example, there is a sentiment in some parts of contemporary society that, "back in the day", issues like race and gender were never a problem and that the new generation is making things more difficult than they ought to be. There is a parallel here to the criticism that is often levelled at psychotherapy itself: that facing our wounds will only make them worse. Both cases represent an investment in the strategy of denial. In today's society, many dialogues are emerging about issues that have previously been denied, which are bringing with them a lot of pain and discomfort. However, this is not the creation of a new problem; it is the return of difficulties that have long been denied. It reflects the fact that there is hope and that the conditions that are needed for integration, which were not there before, may now be found. Yet, in order for healing to happen, these wounds and this pain must be understood and felt. The boundaries of denial that have been used to wall off and oppress the parts of our society that have been suffering must be dissolved. For somebody who has had the privilege of not having to carry these wounds, encountering this pain will be a new experience that they will naturally want to push away. This is why, often when white people are exposed to the reality of racism, or cis-gendered people to the difficulties facing transgender people, it can feel to them like a problem is being created, rather than being resolved.

In the same way that the "Self" has an intelligence beyond our conscious awareness, perhaps our collective psyche too, has a hidden capacity to reconnect itself that lies beyond our understanding. The symptoms and sufferings that we face in our modern times may not only be catastrophes, but might also be a call to love: an opportunity for healing. Just as in the process of attending to our personal traumas in psychotherapy, we need to listen to the voices of the parts of society that are in pain and need. By opening up to their suffering and vulnerability, we can bridge the fissures that exist between us. In this way, our pain can be what connects, rather than divides, us.

Summary

The ways in which we have learnt to protect our unmet needs form a hard protective layer that conceals our vulnerability from view. When we understand this, we are able to see through the prickly exterior of others and glimpse the vulnerability below that longs for connection. This can transform our perception of the ill will of others to a recognition that difficult behaviours are often understandable adaptations for survival that protect unmet needs and vulnerabilities. When we view the world in this way, a compassionate attitude naturally follows. The process of connecting with our vulnerability begins with our symptoms and suffering that signal the awakening of our dormant trauma, calling on us to seek the help we need. Whilst this can feel like a painful process, it reflects the fact that our unconscious mind has sensed the possibility for connection—a process that is mirrored in how society begins to process its collective denial and trauma. Whilst facing our wounds may feel like a descent into the abyss, it is, in fact, a journey of recovery and healing for the parts of ourselves that are in the greatest need.

CHAPTER 9

Embracing dependency

In order to break down the walls of denial that have kept us safe but disconnected, we must open up to others and allow ourselves to be vulnerable. However, this brings with it the potential for both pain and healing, leaving our hope and denial to wrestle for control over our fate. Our denial compels us with shame to keep our vulnerability hidden and safe. Hope, on the other hand, encourages us to make a leap of faith, trusting that we will be caught by another. In taking this risk, not only can we find deeper and more fulfilling connections with others, but we can also discover a profound sense of enduring security by transforming our inner relationships.

Kaitlin

To illustrate the process of embracing our vulnerability, we will now return to Kaitlin, whom we last discussed in Chapter 4, to follow her through the rest of her therapy journey. Kaitlin, as you may remember, was struggling with feelings of jealousy in her relationship with her partner, George. Since the session described in Chapter 4, Kaitlin was beginning to understand how her jealousy played a role in protecting her vulnerability by pushing others away whenever she felt the threat of abandonment. She had also started talking to me more about her early teenage years and her parents' divorce. She described how, when her father moved out, her mother became prone to outbursts of anger or would become upset whenever Kaitlin would mention him. Kaitlin soon learnt not to talk about her father, nor to express any emotion that might indicate the distress that she was feeling. In the absence of somebody that she could share her feelings with, Kaitlin put her own emotional reality on hold and, instead, convinced herself that she was actually unfazed by her parents' divorce. As she began to talk about this difficult time in therapy, her distress came back to her as if remembering a long-forgotten bad dream.

Client—Kaitlin (K) and Therapist—Joseph (J)

K: I couldn't really mention anything to my mum either …

J: And your dad?

K: No (*she sighs and laughs gently*) … he was off totally. Well … I did see him, but he wasn't really there … if that makes sense. Not emotionally available, as they say.

J: Ah … so no-one you could really talk to.

K: Yeah …

J: And meanwhile you're having to pretend everything's okay.

K: Yeah … when it's not. (*Her lip trembles for a moment, and then she sits more upright.*) I guess I felt like I'd just have to look after myself from here on in.

J: Like, no matter how upset you got, you'd just have to deal with it on your own.

K: Yeah … and … I don't want to … I don't know (*she is holding back tears*). I have this hard lump in my throat …

J: Like it's stuck?

K: Yeah … like it wants to come out.

J: What would happen if you let it? (*I lean in slightly.*)

K: I don't know. (*She looks tense for a moment.*)

J: (*I notice my body is also tense. I sit back in my chair slightly and feel my body relax as I do so.*) Maybe that's a tricky question … you're always welcome to cry, or however you want to express yourself, you don't have to explain. (*I notice that I feel quite exposed saying this, as though I have momentarily discarded a persona that I didn't even realise I was inhabiting.*)

K: Thanks … (*Her lip shakes and tears fill her eyes.*)

J: (*Time begins to feel as though it is slowing down, and I feel my vision soften. A warm tingling sensation fills my chest. My senses feel acutely heightened, and yet I feel a calm spaciousness too.*)

K: (*She looks at me for a moment before closing her eyes suddenly, as if wincing. Her body shrinks back into the chair, and she begins to sob, rocking back and forth. Her arms are pulled into her sides, and her hands are opening and closing slightly, as if she is grasping at the air.*)

J: (*I realise that I'm nodding and rocking slowly in my chair too.*)

K: (*She looks up again and we share another brief moment of eye contact before she lets herself fall back into her chair, crying even deeper now.*)

Breaking down can become breaking through when there is someone there to hold us as we fall apart. For Kaitlin, this was a moment where she could let go of the ways in which she had been holding herself together and holding her tears back. Instead, she allowed herself to be held by another. Her grief had broken through, out of its isolation, and could finally be felt, experienced, and receive the care that it needed. However, before she took that risk, Kaitlin had to overcome the shame that had kept her longing hidden and safe from the threat of rejection.

To overcome denial and the shame that keeps it in place, we need to be able to trust someone enough to open up to them and expose our vulnerability. In the time leading up to this session, Kaitlin had been able to experience first-hand in therapy how her emotional needs and vulnerabilities had felt welcome and were not rejected. Over time, the trust that had been built brought to the surface both the previously buried hope that she may be able to fully express her grief and the shame that surrounded this need. As this shame arose and Kaitlin became conscious of it, she was able to identify the emotional conviction at the root of the denial of her need for others: "If I become vulnerable and express my emotions, the other person will punish me or push me away."

Denial and shame are at their most powerful when we are unaware of them. But when we receive the acceptance of others, we become more able to accept ourselves and our hidden needs, no longer having to hide from our shame. In doing so, we can begin to see more clearly the stories that our denial is telling us and therefore find more freedom to choose whether or not we continue to abide by their narratives. In becoming aware of her belief that her vulnerability would be rejected, along with feeling increasing acceptance of her need for others, Kaitlin was able to break free of the compulsion to keep her vulnerability hidden and instead express herself in the way that she needed to. Through this experience, Kaitlin was able to digest the overwhelming grief that she had been unable to express at the time of her parents' divorce. This process would continue in the following months of therapy as she was able to find new meanings and put into words the experience that she had gone through and the impact it had on how she perceived relationships.

The body knows

As babies, our psychological and physical needs are almost inseparable. To be held as a baby is to be both "held in mind" and to be held close to another body. To be mirrored, seen, soothed, or given warmth are as much physical needs as they are psychological ones. As we grow older, the stories that we develop give us a sense of separation between mind and body, and between self and other. Our deepest relational needs, however, are our earliest, originating at a time in our development before we experience these divisions. As a result, these most fundamental needs can feel as though they threaten to unravel our most basic psychological constructs and expose us in our greatest state of vulnerability. Likewise, we can come to feel ashamed of our bodies and their impulses because they seem to lay bare our most fundamental needs. Whilst denial hides our needs by ring-fencing them with alternative narratives, it is shame that descends on our bodies to suppress our most primal longings.

In order to restore a feeling of security to her relationships, Kaitlin needed the experience of being held as she grieved. Yet her deepest need had become the source of her greatest shame. It was shame that Kaitlin had felt in the tightening lump in her throat as she edged closer to expressing her grief. This was the manifestation of her psychological conflict at a bodily level: a physical experience of holding in her cries. When I had asked her "What would happen if you let it? (come out)", she had looked tense. In trying to engage this bodily process with words, asking for an explanation, rather than an expression, the result was jarring. However, when I was able to embody a state of receptivity and "openness", Kaitlin was able to release her grief, trusting that I was going to receive and hold her as she disintegrated into her feelings. It is hard to put into words exactly what being "open" means, as it is more than just a mental state alone. It is to be in a tender state of receptivity that is communicated mostly subconsciously, through our body language and presence, rather than through our words. It is the willingness to allow someone else's experience to truly move us. In order to do so, we need to be in touch with our own capacity to feel, so that we are able to receive another's feelings and allow them to resonate with us deeply. To "open" to another, whether sharing our pain or receiving someone else's, is to allow ourselves to be vulnerable and to let someone else touch us deeply. As Mary Oliver writes in "Wild geese":[35]

> You do not have to walk on your knees
> for a hundred miles through the desert repenting.
> You only have to let the soft animal of your body
> love what it loves.
> Tell me about despair, yours, and I will tell you mine.

As Oliver suggests, our bodies have a simple, hidden wisdom. When we allow ourselves to open up, they know what to do: whether that is to burst into tears or to reach out and hold someone close. When we inhabit our bodies, rather than the maps and templates in our minds, our expressions can flow instinctually and find the connections that they need. For Kaitlin, this meant being able to express the tears of her grief. Whilst for myself, when I dropped my ideas about what the right thing to say was and instead opened up to the present moment with my own vulnerability, I was able to embody the open receptivity that Kaitlin needed. These are, of course, both relational expressions; they do not happen in isolation, but rather occur in response to one another. When we are vulnerable, we call forth the tenderness of others, opening up the connection between us.

Whilst shame may try to hinder our connection to one another with its uncomfortable sensations that discourage awareness of our bodies and their needs, we can break free from its grip by fully inhabiting our somatic experience. By allowing ourselves to feel the physical sensations that shame brings, we avoid getting carried away by its narratives. Instead, we can return to the feelings and needs that reside within our bodies. Keeping our awareness faithful to our sensory experience is the remedy to denial and along with the presence of a caring and supportive other, the means by which we can get back in touch with the vulnerability that our shame denies.

When we shut out our dependent needs, we disconnect from their source: the body. Our bodies are the root of our experience, the ground of our sensation and our gateway to receiving the world. When we hide from our needs and desires, distancing ourselves from our sensations, we avoid our most vivid and alive capacity in which to relate to the world. As a result, things can come to feel flat or depressed, even. Our need and desire for others is our stimulus to vitality and aliveness. When we can open to the experience of our bodies, we can be in touch with our own being at its most essential level: our present experience. When we allow ourselves to be vulnerable in this way, we are renewed and invigorated by life itself: the wild mystery that lies beyond the stories and templates that shelter us. When we see the world as it is, unfiltered by our preconceptions and untouched by our understanding that freezes it in place, we experience life outside of our templates of "self" and "other", with the awe and wonder of a newborn baby.

Holding

Being held is dependency embodied. It is the physical expression of being totally supported by another person. Just as when we are physically held, we can relax all the muscles that we use to hold our shape, when we are psychologically held, we can let go of maintaining our sense of self. Our sense of self is an ongoing narrative that acts like a container, drawing a boundary around "us" so that we feel separate and together. When we are held, we can release this story momentarily, letting another person act as the container for us.

This allows us to become what is inside the container: to explore our feelings, experiences, and memories in a raw state without having to distort them in order to fit them into our pre-existing stories and templates.

In psychotherapy, a therapist "holds" their client in two main ways: through the relationship that is established, as described earlier, and through the therapy arrangement itself, which is often known as the "frame".[36] The "frame" is everything that defines the therapy relationship: the consistent weekly hour, the cancellation policy, confidentiality, and all the other boundaries that define the space. Upholding, maintaining, and taking care of these parameters is what helps to create an environment that can be depended upon, freeing the client to let go of having to take care of anything within the therapy space. This allows the client to release the ways in which they hold themselves together and, instead, embody their dependent needs. The solid walls of a container allow what is inside to become liquid whilst still holding its shape. The containing environment of psychotherapy enables a client to relinquish their own structure: the walls of denial and the stories and templates that insulate them from both their own experience and from others. Walled-off "lumps" of indigestible trauma can be dissolved and mixed again with the rest of their fluid experience. From inside the sheltered safety of therapy, a client can rebuild their own container, the story of their "self", using the raw material from their expanded experience to construct a "self" that is more whole and permeable to the outside world. Like a caterpillar turning into a butterfly, it is the cocoon that enables the caterpillar to dissolve and for a process of transformation to take place. Just like babies, we need to be held by others in order to grow.

Knocking on the door

Our inner relationships are a mirror of our outer ones. As we develop throughout our lives, we internalise the relationships that we have with those around us, and they become part of the make-up of our selves. We relate to ourselves in the same way in which we have been related to. For example, when Kaitlin's mother rejected her vulnerability, Kaitlin learnt to reject her own vulnerability. Likewise, in experiencing her vulnerability being accepted in therapy, she was able to subsequently accept her own vulnerability. When we are looked after and cared for by another, we learn how to care for ourselves. A new inner relationship is formed, one within which we are able to provide for ourselves some of the warmth and understanding that we have received. That being said, self-sufficiency will never be a replacement for being cared for by others. The self-love we carry is an echo of the love that we have been shown. Whilst we can pass it on to others, it cannot sustain us forever, and we will always depend on others in some way. To visualise how intertwined these inner and outer relationships are, let us return to the story from Chapter 4 of the crying boy who was sent to his bedroom to cry alone—although this time, the story starts just after he is sent to his room.

> Muffled sounds of crying can be heard from the upstairs bedroom as the father continues to work downstairs. When his wife comes home, he is withdrawn and cold, unable to share his feelings or talk about how his day went. Instead, this unspoken distance boils over into an argument. He storms off back into the study, locking himself away.
>
> A crisis point has been reached. A new story is needed. There is, and always will be, a different narrative living somewhere under one roof. Here, this story finds a voice in a gentle knock on the study door. "Are you okay?" she asks. Her vulnerable openness melts his anger, and a hug is shared. Something softens.
>
> Shortly after, the father goes upstairs and knocks on the door. "Are you okay?" he says. The little boy is scared and unsure. "No," he says, his voice wavering. "I'm sorry I shouted at you earlier … your knee, it must have really hurt," the father says as his heart breaks. The door opens, and the teary-eyed boy stands at the doorway. The father hugs his son.

We, too, must knock on the door of our exiled vulnerability. This is as much a door inside us as it is the door of another. When we reach out for help, we are also reaching inwards towards the parts of ourselves that need our love. When our abandoned selves are embraced, they will no longer need to feel rejected or to cry alone. Instead, when we turn towards them, they will feel welcomed and wanted. In this embrace, we foster an unconditional acceptance of ourselves that soothes our fears of abandonment. Accepting ourselves more fully also comes hand-in-hand with a greater capacity to embrace the world just as it is. When we are able to more fully accept the totality of ourselves and the world in their whole and diverse natures, we experience a profound sense of peace and find the sense of security that we have been seeking all along.

Changing relationships

In the beginning, it was the search for love that had brought Kaitlin to psychotherapy. Since starting her therapy journey, Kaitlin had discovered that in opening up to another and to herself, she was able to find a newfound sense of aliveness, wholeness, and security. In many ways, she had already discovered within herself much of what she had hoped to find in a romantic relationship. However, unlike her previous "avoidant" self-sufficiency, this inner resource did not become a substitute to avoid the difficulties of an outer relationship, but rather supported Kaitlin in opening up to others.

Kaitlin's relationship with George became stronger over the next few years, and her experiences of jealousy diminished with the sense of inner trust that she found in her commitment to being ever-present to her own needs and vulnerabilities. Whilst she was able to feel safe and have many of her needs met in her relationship with George, her relationship with him was no longer her sole hope for finding the care that she longed for, which contributed to making the relationship less volatile. Furthermore, now that she was on speaking terms with her own vulnerability, it would no longer appear out of nowhere in outbursts of anger or jealousy. Kaitlin found that she was increasingly able to be in touch with her own feelings and regulate her emotions inwardly. Also, as she became more comfortable opening up to others, she found that she was able to express herself more deeply and be met and cared for in the ways in which she truly needed and desired. She could cry more openly, say how she really felt, and ask for what she wanted and needed. This enabled Kaitlin to find more depth, connection, regulation, and fulfilment in both her relationship with George and in the other relationships in her life. Of course, this was not a straightforward process. As she risked being more vulnerable, she also opened herself up to experiencing the difficult feelings of rejection and abandonment that arose when her hopes and needs were not met. However, Kaitlin's capacity to be present with these feelings had grown, having had the experience of digesting them in the presence of another. Where her experience of abandonment had previously lived behind a wall of denial as trauma, it now existed as an unpleasant, but ultimately bearable and manageable feeling that no longer secretly controlled her behaviour.

Too much?

"Can we be too dependent on others?" I often hear concerned voices ask. More often than not, this question is triggered by our personal and cultural fears of dependency. Nevertheless, it is worth exploring the nature of being "too dependent" as it is such a frequent response when discussing dependency. In order to do so, let us consider "a person who depends on others too much", somebody who might be labelled "lazy" or "emotionally needy". This kind of learnt helplessness can arise in all sorts of contexts, whether it is in a romantic relationship, a family dynamic, or within the context of our society. Either way, let us begin by considering the developmental origins of a person who has learnt that their needs are better met when they do not exercise their autonomy or independence and instead rely solely on others.

As we develop, autonomy is nurtured when a carer sensitively responds to an infant's needs, letting the infant first reach out into the world to try to find what they need and then responding appropriately. However, when the response is either too quick, too slow, not enough or too much, the infant's relationship to their sense of agency is disturbed.[37] For example, when a baby is fed before they have a chance to feel hungry or to seek out feeding for themselves, the infant misses out on the experience of finding what they need themselves. In response, the infant will adapt, changing themselves and sacrificing their own sensory experience in order to align with the care that they are being given. This results in their connection to their deeper feelings and needs becoming distant and dysregulated, which may result in them losing touch with their own creativity, power and self-direction.

When somebody has become estranged from their own self and therefore reliant on others, there is an unmet requirement to have their autonomy, their self, nurtured through attuned responsiveness and mirroring. In fact, we all need to have the quiet and hidden voices of what we really think and feel, heard and reflected back to us to strengthen our connection to the senses of our body and our own creative being. In order to get back in touch with ourselves, we need others. A person who "depends on others too much" requires an attuned other in order to develop their independence. Independence arises from dependency: it is something that we must find in, not outside of, relationship with others.

The privilege of care

What if there is no one to care for us? What about those who cannot afford the privilege of psychotherapy? There are no easy answers to these questions, and it is unfair but true that those who may be in the most need are often those who are least likely to receive help. This is a tragic injustice. Having said that, whilst psychotherapy may be an ideal environment to receive psychological support, it is of course not the only place where the understanding, warmth and "holding" that we need can be found. There are many different ways in which we may experience being held in the care of another: a partner, friend, family member, or even a teacher who sees us, a shopkeeper who treats us with respect and dignity, or simply a kind smile from a stranger. Small acts of kindness, care, and openness circulate between us all the time. Of course, receiving love and kindness from another is a kind of privilege in itself, and there are those who have to survive on very little care from others. Just like the darkest corners of our inner worlds, as a society, we often collectively disconnect from the most intense sufferings of the world. It is these least privileged parts that exist in the darkness of denial, both inside and outside of ourselves, that we must turn towards and embrace. This is not simply a moral duty; it is to face the reality of our interdependent wholeness.

Summary

In the presence of a caring and trusting relationship, we can open up to one another and risk becoming vulnerable. Standing in the way of this connection is our denial, which hides the unmet needs that reside in our bodies with the uncomfortable sensations of shame. When the needs we struggle to accept in ourselves are met with acceptance by others, we are helped to face our shame and free ourselves from its restrictions, allowing our needs to flow instinctively towards fulfilment. Our deepest and most primal of these needs originate in our earliest and greatest states of dependency, where the mind and body are one. The most fundamental of all these needs is to be held. In psychotherapy, being held allows us to let go of the stories we use to hold ourselves together so that we are able to explore our experience more directly and find new narratives that are more inclusive of our wholeness. Even more fundamentally, being held enables us to open up, exposing our most tender wounds and allowing them to be expressed, touched, and transformed. Not only does this process enrich our outer relationships, but it heals our inner ones too. Being accepted and fully accepting ourselves gives us a sense of security that our denial can never match. Unfortunately, being cared for by another is a blessing that is not evenly distributed throughout our society. Turning towards the suffering that exists both within and around us is the path to greater wholeness, a journey we will explore in the next chapter.

CHAPTER 10

Discovering our interdependent nature

Our wounds are doorways to greater connection. When we try to shelter ourselves from the suffering of the world by seeking refuge in our separateness, we are inadvertently cutting ourselves off from the richness of life. However, when we face our pain and helplessness, rather than deny it, we can rediscover the treasure of our interdependent wholeness that lies beneath. In telling stories that reveal our interconnected nature, rather than conceal it, we can be supported by our interdependence, rather than being threatened by it.

Facing our pain

> You can hold yourself back from the sufferings of the world, that is something you are free to do and it accords with your nature, but perhaps this very holding back is the one suffering you could avoid. (Franz Kafka)[38]

The threads that connect us lie suspended between all things like an infinite spider's web.[39] These connections are the basis of our interdependent reality and the channels through which we are joined to each other. When these channels are open, we are vulnerable, exposed to both the joy and pain that the totality of our being brings.

However, when this suffering becomes overwhelming or unbearable, we constrict and knot our connections, closing them off with our denial and becoming wounded. The more we allow ourselves to truly care, to open to our connections and to love, the more we expose ourselves to the inevitable letdowns, losses, and heartaches that life entails. Yet, it is through opening to our connections that we can receive the joy and purpose that love can bring. Whilst loving may expose us to pain, it fills our lives with meaning, which ultimately makes bearing our suffering feel worthwhile. We will no doubt suffer, but as Kafka says, perhaps we do not also have to endure the pain of "holding back" from and denying our suffering, cutting ourselves off from the connection, depth, meaning, and love that are inseparable from it.

In order to be able to heal the wounds of our disconnection, we have to face our denial and bear the suffering that we have been hiding from. We must turn towards each other, as in doing so, we can both give and receive the support that we need to tend to the pain we carry. Connecting more deeply with others is inseparable from reconnecting more deeply with ourselves. As we embrace the tenderness of our own vulnerability, our capacity to be present to the suffering of others will also grow, and we will no longer need to deny the pain or injustice in the world in order to cope. When we face our wounds, we are attending to the very threads that join us, unpicking the knots of our denial and opening the channels that connect us to all things. In doing so, we increasingly perceive the interdependent wholeness that is ultimately our greatest source of support.

No one to forgive

The threads that connect us do not just link us together as individuals, but bind the totality of everything together. We are inextricably tangled up and connected to the fate, myths, and wounds of our society and world. The stories of our culture are mirror images of the stories that we tell ourselves to protect ourselves from our own wounds and shame. In the same way that we avoid our personal pain with denial, our culture shields us from pain by telling stories that give us a sense of separation from the most difficult aspects of our suffering world. Often, these narratives of separation mean that we come to see our world as divided, projecting our own suffering and guilt onto others, blaming them, and distancing ourselves from pain. In order to rediscover a sense of mutuality, of wholeness, both as individuals and as a culture, we need to learn to see through the stories that split us apart—to forgive.

> Loose the cords of mistakes binding us, as we release the strands we hold of others' guilt.[40]

This is Neil Douglas-Klotz's translation and interpretation of the passage in the Lord's prayer usually translated as "Forgive us our sins, as we forgive those that sin against us". To forgive is to loosen our tightened grip on the cords that bind us, freeing our connection from being throttled. It is the process of untangling the mess and confusion that we create with the stories we weave to hide from our pain. As we let go of the threads of the stories we hold, we unravel our notions of separateness and, in doing so, untangle the shame and guilt that we are caught in. Zhuangzi illustrates how it is in our notions of "self" and "other" that we get ensnared in anger and blame.

> If a man, having lashed two hulls together, is crossing a river, and an empty boat happens along and bumps into him, no matter how hot tempered the man may be, he will not get angry. But if there should be someone in the other boat, then he will shout out to haul this way or veer that. If his first shout is not heeded, he will shout again, and if that is not heard, he will shout a third time, this time with a torrent of curses following. In the first instance, he wasn't angry; now in the second, he is. Earlier he faced emptiness, now he faces occupancy. If a man could succeed in making himself empty and, in that way, wander through the world, then who could do him harm? (Zhuangzi)[41]

Forgiving others is inseparable from forgiving ourselves. In order to quell our blame, hate, and anger, we must see through the illusions of our separate sense of self. When we understand that there is no singular centre that has control over all that we do, then, there is no one to point the finger at: no self to feel deficient, corrupted, or ashamed and no other to blame. The more we view ourselves and others as empty boats, as the unfolding of past contexts playing themselves out in the present, the more we are able to perceive the totality of our interdependency. It is impossible to single out and separate any one part of our whole and interconnected nature to blame. We are all products of the world around us: of both the care that we have been given and the wounds that we have received. When we see ourselves through the lens of our interconnected nature, we cannot help but view the world from a non-judgemental and compassionate attitude of forgiveness.

It is not easy to forgive, however. When we feel as though somebody has hurt us, forgiveness can feel impossible. To forgive is to feel the pain that we have been holding ourselves apart from with the stories that keep it at arm's length. As we have explored, bearing pain is something that we need others to help us with. We need to be understood and forgiven by others in order to forgive ourselves. Psychotherapy, in this light, is a journey to find forgiveness. It is the process of understanding the string of contexts of our past from which we weave our stories of "self" and "other". In doing so, we unravel the narratives of guilt and blame that we have fashioned from our experiences. Together, we bring compassion, understanding, and company to the experiences that we have previously had to carry alone. In psychotherapy, we unpick the psychological knots that disconnect us from one another, opening ourselves up to our interconnected wholeness as a result. The more we understand about ourselves and others, the more we will see that we are all the same and that we only appear to be different because of the different contexts in which we are reflected. The more we are truly open to seeing our interconnection with others, the more we will discover an ever-increasing sense of mutuality and kinship with the rest of the world.

Forgiving injustice

When we forgive, we are able to see more clearly our connection to the rest of the world and the tragedy of the pain that we are caught in. As we untangle the stories that keep us separate, we must confront the injustices that exist between us. This means facing each other's pain and comprehending our larger contexts without getting stuck in the stories that divide us. For those of us in a position of privilege, this means understanding the full circumstances of our advantages and taking responsibility for the position in which we now stand. Being privileged often means that we have benefited from structures in society that are unjust, or that have been unjust in the past. Facing these injustices means facing the stories of denial within our culture that justify inequality and deny the pain of others. In order to relinquish these stories, we must open ourselves to the suffering we have been ignoring and bear the guilt that we may feel. Denial thrives on guilt, blame, and shame; therefore, we must be able to forgive if we are to attend to the wounds that sit between us.

Only when we are not locked into our ideas of "self" and "other" can we face our collective guilt and pain together. We must take accountability for our boats, our "selves", without falling into the illusion that they are all that we really are and losing sight of our whole nature. This is the distinction between taking responsibility for ourselves and "identifying" with the story of our "self" too literally. Taking responsibility is being willing to be accountable for the identities we are connected to, even though we may know that they are not truly representative of our whole self. In the same way that we must take responsibility for the actions of our past, even though there is no continuous self that truly transcends time, we must take stewardship of the chains of contexts, stories, and identities that we find ourselves a part of. For example, as a white person, this means facing the reality of the wounds that racism causes, owning the role that white people have played, and continue to play, in upholding racial injustice, and embracing the responsibility to help dismantle it. If we lose sight of the totality of our interdependent wholeness and instead identify too closely with our identities and stories, in this case as a "white person", we will feel compelled to defend our identities from blame and fall back into the more separate sense of self that our stories of denial create. When we can see the world as a sea of empty boats bumping into each other, free from our ideas of self and other, we will not be preoccupied with pointing fingers and instead will be more available to get on with bailing water out of the vessels that are most in need.

The gift of the wound

Entrust your wound to a Teacher's care.
Flies gather there—those self-protecting feelings,
your attachment to what seems yours.

> Let a Teacher brush away the flies
> and dress the wound with care.
> Do not look away—keep gazing at
> the bandaged place—that's where the Light enters.
> And don't delude yourself you're healing alone.
> (Jalal al-Din Muhammad Rumi)[42]

Beneath the self-protective stories of our denial lie the painful wounds of our disturbed connections. Yet, this is not all that remains hidden. Buried even deeper still, within and beyond our most painful wounds, resides our most precious treasure: our union with the totality of our interdependent being. In the helplessness, powerlessness, and pain of our wounds, our illusions of self-sufficiency and separateness are brought to their knees. In being pushed to the limits of our "self", we are faced with what lies beyond. We are forced to confront the full extent of our utter dependence on the world and recognise how inextricably we are bound to it. From this most vulnerable position, naked and without the clothes of separation that our denial comforts us with, we are poised to catch a glimpse of the staggering beauty of our greater interconnected nature.

As we relinquish our denial and welcome back the parts of our greater wholeness that we have shut out, we are gifted with their unique riches. Just as the vulnerability we deny has the power to enrich our emotional lives, every part of our being, even those that we struggle to accept, holds a unique value to offer. Often, it is the most difficult aspects of life that give us the greatest rewards: just ask a parent! Perhaps one of the hardest parts of the already difficult task of raising a child is responding to challenging behaviour. Even so, a good parent will endeavour to try to understand their child's behaviour in terms of an attempt at growth. This is an extremely worthwhile effort, as a child's greatest gift is often intertwined with their deepest need, representing their most unique and challenging point of growth. Imagine a "naughty" child in class, disrupting the others and "fooling around". At first glance, it is easy to just see "bad" behaviour. Although if we spend some time understanding the child, perhaps we will discover that they are simply bored due to being very intelligent and therefore unstimulated. Or perhaps their unique ability to engage others or make them laugh is an underappreciated talent they may later bring to fruition as a comedian or performer. Yet, so often, what will happen is that these aptitudes will go unrecognised and instead the child will be punished, leaving their gifts to go undiscovered and un-nurtured. Where there is difficulty and wounding, there is unacknowledged potential. Our job is to try to see the world with the same compassionate attempt at understanding that a loving parent has for their child. When we are presented with difficult facets of life, if we approach them with the possibility in mind that perhaps there is something that we are not fully understanding, we can find hidden riches in even the darkest and most unacceptable places.

Of all the challenging aspects of life, those of pain, suffering, and heartbreak have to be some of the most difficult to accept. What purpose do they serve, and what value could possibly be hidden inside them? Whilst pain can force us to turn away from the world and close off our connections with denial, it can also be the force that softens our hearts and opens us up to greater depth and intimacy in our connection with others. Hidden behind our suffering, just beneath the surface of our vulnerability, is the gift of tenderness. Tenderness is inseparable from our capacity to feel sad, hurt, low, and heartbroken. Yet, it is also what allows our spirit to soar and our hearts to sing. We can only be moved to tears by the beauty of poetry as easily as we can be by the grief of our world. Our tenderness is our capacity to feel: to be touched and moved by life. It also gives us our ability to love and care for others. Tenderness is the very foundation of compassion, and by opening to our pain, we are opening to a greater capacity to love and be loved.

Our true nature

The climate crisis may be the most profound expression of our disconnection from our interdependent nature. In order to avoid confronting our dependency, we have "self-sabotaged" our relationship to the environment, denying our reliance on it and attacking the source of our care. We have lost sight of the aliveness of our world, rending it into a lifeless void so that we can justify the way that we treat it. Despite this tragedy, the extent of our wounded relationship to the Earth is surpassed by the value of the treasure hidden beneath: our true nature. The climate crisis is the symptom that brings our modern world to therapy, where we must work through the trauma of our disconnection, rewrite the myths that we live by, and rediscover the depth of our greater wholeness.

When we recognize the environment as a living other rather than an inanimate object, we must confront the pain and damage caused by our denial and disconnection. Whilst the climate crisis is most often framed in terms of the destruction and suffering it will cause to humanity, this still reflects a denial of nature's subjectivity and intrinsic value, as if it is only the consequences for our society that truly matter. Only when we approach the environment with an understanding that it *is* "us", not with the view of what "we" can get from "it", will we be able to truly meet the depth of this wound. Paradoxically, by letting in the "otherness" of nature, opening ourselves up to its foreign agency, we can discover that we are, in fact, inseparable from it.

> I am something the earth does. When I stand among the trees, I realise that I have grown upwards as they have, their out-breath is my in-breath, my in-breath their out-breath. I did not come into the world, I came out of it. (Tenjo Hopwood)[43]

The human race is not a separate "other" that is in opposition to nature. The human race is nature: we are a part of its ecosystem. Our perception of our separateness, however, perpetuates our sense of guilt and shame, making the wound of our disturbed relationship to the environment harder to face. This is analogous to the sense of shame we internalise around the traumas we face as we grow up and the way in which we blame ourselves for how we have been let down by others. In this case, it is the "empty boats" of the stories of our cultures that have let us down and led to our disconnected attitudes and actions towards the environment. Healing our traumatic connection to the environment is not a matter of berating ourselves or others, but rather, forgiving, which means seeing through the stories of separateness that lead to our shame, guilt, pain, and the environmental crisis itself.

In discovering again our greater nature, there are glorious and indescribable rewards to be found. When we see the world as being alive and valuable, we see that we are surrounded by and submerged in an infinite web of living beauty. There is an endless depth in nature that is so desperately needed to feed the meaning-starved landscape of our modern culture. Nature is a living representation of the wholeness of our interdependency: its ecosystems are demonstrations of the inherent balance and completeness of the wholeness of our "Self". Nature demonstrates to us that every little thing has a role, function, and purpose that is needed. If we see something in the natural world that we think is merely superfluous, it reflects the fact that we do not yet understand the gift that is being given. Our connection to our environment is synonymous with our connection to the wholeness of our interdependent being, and ultimately, it is impossible to describe the value or appearance of this treasure. Although, perhaps in some rare moments, we can catch a glimpse of it.

> To see a World in a Grain of Sand
> And a Heaven in a Wild Flower
> Hold Infinity in the palm of your hand
> And Eternity in an hour
> (William Blake)[44]

Being supported

We come to our denial through our search for safety. Yet, by trying to find security through independence and control, we inadvertently make our anxieties worse. To be in denial is to turn away from the threads that connect us and, instead, to look to our stories of separateness for reassurance. However, we will never find the security we seek in our denial, as whilst we may ignore and constrict the channels that connect us, we cannot sever them. Our connection to one another will always be there, subconsciously reminding us of our vulnerability. When we turn against our dependency and vulnerability, the interdependent nature of reality becomes a threat to the stories we tell ourselves. It is only by allowing ourselves to face our wholeness that we will not be at war with our greater interdependency. In embracing the pain of our vulnerability and dependency, we can find a more enduring sense of security. When we can truly let go of the narratives that keep us separate, we will find that our interdependency is the very thing that holds us up.

Let us imagine for a moment just how supported we are. Above us shines a sun that keeps everything growing, providing the food and warmth we need to survive. Beneath us, the ground is holding up our bodies. Every day we use cars, roads, houses, phones, all built with the genius, blood, sweat, and tears of others. Our ancestors have toiled since the beginning of time, each nurturing the next generation to carry us here. Our past selves have been through the difficult process of living in order to bring us into this present moment. Our bodies are working tirelessly to keep us going, breathing, metabolising, digesting, and renewing themselves. Even our thoughts are working to support us by planning, calculating, and navigating a passage for us through time. When we relinquish the sense of a separate self, there is nothing in existence but an endless outpouring of support.

Telling new stories

One of the potential rewards of psychotherapy is to become more aware of the narratives that we have learnt about ourselves and others from our upbringing and culture. This gives us the opportunity to re-evaluate what stories and templates serve ourselves and our communities, and which ones we would be better off without. When we are able to identify the maps we are living by, we can hold them less tightly and therefore be more open to our actual present experience and its interdependent richness. When we widen our perspective in this way, we have more space to understand others and contemplate how they see the world without feeling like our own narratives are being threatened. This quality is particularly important for a psychotherapist to possess, but it equally benefits us all by allowing us to open up to each other with less fear, fostering a sense of kinship and belonging, and helping us feel a greater sense of existential security.

Whilst our stories and the ways we hold onto them can unintentionally divide us, there are times when we need a good story to take refuge in. But what makes a good story? A good story resists us clinging to it too fiercely, providing us shelter without requiring us to grasp it single-mindedly. It makes room for everyone, the totality of our inner and outer worlds, so that we do not have to split ourselves or exile others to maintain its integrity. It highlights the vulnerability of others and does not demonise them, so that we can relate to them with understanding and compassion. A good story does not lose sight of our need for others, so that we do not get lost in the illusions of self-sufficiency and independence. It reflects the depth of our greater nature as much as possible; the profundity of its meaning can thus match the extent of our suffering. A good story reveals, rather than hides, our connection to each other and the world beyond.

Summary

We deny our connections due to the pain that they bring. However, in doing so, we constrict the channels through which we give and receive the love and support that makes our suffering bearable. When we close off our connections and instead seek refuge in stories of separateness, we get tangled up in knots of denial, blame, and guilt. To forgive is to see through the illusion of this separate existence and recognise that there is no "self" or "other" to blame, which allows us to take more responsibility for our place in the world and attend to the injustices that sit between us. Behind every wound lies an exiled portion of our wholeness, carrying a gift that can enrich our lives. In our pain, there is tenderness and compassion. Concealed within the climate crisis is our connection to nature, the most tangible way in which we can relate to the mystery and beauty of our interdependent wholeness. As we bear the pain of these wounds together, we have the opportunity of retelling the stories that have kept us safe but separate, and weaving new ones that connect us and tell of our interdependent mystery. When we embrace our interdependency instead of denying it, our connection to all things does not feel like a threat but can, in fact, be what supports us.

Conclusion

We are living in a time of crisis. Whilst the problems that we face as a society seem to be driving us apart, they also hold the potential to bring us together. Just like the difficulties we encounter in our day-to-day relationships, we can either face the connections that expose our vulnerability and pain or turn away in denial. If we keep investing in denial and the false sense of security it offers through its stories of separateness and independence, we will carry on wounding the very bonds that sustain us. Alternatively, we can embrace our need for each other and let the challenges and suffering we face reveal the depth and beauty of our true interdependent nature.

To face our dependency is to face our deepest hopes and fears. It is to be reminded of our earliest and most vulnerable moments as babies, where we have not yet formed a sense of "self" and "other". Whilst this union can be blissful, it can also be apocalyptic, as disturbances to our environment crash upon the shores of our senses, shaking us to the core. Once we start to construct the maps and templates that we learn to see ourselves and the world through, we have made our first steps into both self-sufficiency and denial. Every story we adopt offers us some certainty that shelters us from the outside world, at the expense of disconnecting us in some way from a bigger picture. Denial is a storyteller, weaving its narratives in order to exclude anything that would undermine our way of seeing the world or expose us to too much vulnerability or pain. Our dependency falls victim to denial in instances where we have needed others, but have been painfully let down. Denial dresses these wounds with its tales, reassuring us that we can make do without the help of others. However, this coping strategy comes at a price: in denying our need for others, we blame ourselves for our shortfalls and banish our vulnerability with a wall of shame.

When we make an enemy of vulnerability, we turn against anything that threatens to remind us of it, including the very relationships that could provide the care we need. Our anger, commitment issues, addiction, and jealousy are all misguided attempts to protect ourselves from the exposure of needing others. Likewise, when we try to deny our vulnerability by adopting identities based on being superior to others, we exacerbate the narratives of misogyny, racism, and bigotry that perpetuate injustice in our society. Whilst our denial offers us a temporary feeling of safety, by holding us apart from what we fear, it ultimately divides us, exacerbating the insecurity that it seeks to mend. When we try to find safety in independence, we pit ourselves against the interdependent nature of reality. For we are woven inextricably into the fabric of all things in an interconnected web of dependency. Even our sense of a separate "self" is a story that is in denial of the full extent of our interconnection. In order to free ourselves from the prison of our denial, we must face the wounds of our disconnection from which we have been running.

Our vulnerability and dependency hold the key to establishing deeper and more fulfilling relationships with one another. In order to discover the great potential our connections hold, we need to descend into the dark realms of our denial and face the wounds that we have left behind. This is a journey that will seek us out when the time is right. Our subconscious minds have an intelligence beyond our comprehension, and given the right conditions of a warm, responsive, and understanding relationship, will reunite us with the trauma that we have become separated from. Often, this process begins with the arrival of symptoms that might seem to drag us down, but in fact, often lead us to the very places that we need to heal. When we can face our shame, relinquish our protective self-sufficiency, and allow ourselves to be truly open with another person, our wounded vulnerability will instinctively find the connection it needs. The more we are able to open up to others and allow ourselves to be held by them, the deeper the relationship that we can establish with our own vulnerability, which in turn, enriches our lives with its tenderness and vitality. In embracing vulnerability and pain, rather than turning away from it, we are able to foster an unconditional acceptance that can give us a profound sense of security and support that our denial can never match.

The stories that our culture has been telling since the beginning of civilisation have led us down a path of increasing division and alienation. As a species, we have arrived at a point where we are beginning to witness the cost of our illusions of independence and superiority in the breakdown of our environmental systems. The suffering, turmoil, and crises that we face point to the wounds of disconnection that are calling for our attention. Just as in psychotherapy, we must turn towards each other with tender openness and face the pain that blocks our connection. In doing so, not only can we tend to our suffering, but lying just beyond the stories of denial that obscure our view, we can discover the magnificence of our greater interdependent nature.

Notes

Chapter 1 The storms of early dependency

1. Stern, D. N. (1990). *Diary of a Baby: What your Child Sees, Feels, and Experiences*. New York: Basic Books, pp. 31–32.
2. For a full exploration of hope and re-traumatisation in psychotherapy, see Stolorow, R. D., Brandchaft, B., & Atwood, G. E. (1987). *Psychoanalytic Treatment: An Intersubjective Approach*. Hillsdale, NJ: Analytic Press.
3. Winnicott, D. W. (1965). From dependence towards independence in the development of the individual. In: *The Maturational Processes and the Facilitating Environment* (pp. 83–92). London: Karnac, 1990.

Chapter 2 The stories of denial

4. Moriarty, J. (2001). *Nostos: A Return to the Source*. Dublin: Lilliput Press.
5. Joseph Rowntree Foundation (2024). *UK Poverty 2024*. London: Joseph Rowntree Foundation. https://www.jrf.org.uk/uk-poverty-2024-the-essential-guide-to-understanding-poverty-in-the-uk
6. In a study investigating the "Marley hypothesis", which explored how different racial groups have a different perception of current racial inequality, white participants had less knowledge of the historical origins of racism and also perceived less racism in both isolated incidents and systemic manifestations. Nelson, J. C., Adams, G., & Salter, P. S. (2013).

The Marley hypothesis: Denial of racism reflects ignorance of history. *Psychological Science, 24*(2), 213–218.

Chapter 3 The denial of dependency

7. Wilson, W. G. (2019). *Alcoholics Anonymous: The Big Book: The Big Book: The Original 1939 Edition.* New York: Dover Publications.
8. "Self-sabotaging" is based on the ideas of the psychoanalyst Fairbairn and of the "internal saboteur". Fairbairn, W. R. D. (1952). *Psychoanalytic Studies of the Personality.* London: Routledge & Kegan Paul, p. 133.
9. Hoskin, R. A., Blair, K. L., & Holmberg, D. (2024). Femmephobia is a uniquely powerful predictor of anti-gay behavior. *Archives of Sexual Behaviour, 53*(1): 127–140.

Chapter 4 Relationships

10. The client–therapist relationship is also a microcosm of all the therapist's past and present relationships too. However, psychotherapy obviously focuses on exploring the client's contribution to the relationship, not the therapist's. This is, however, why a psychotherapist must develop a good understanding of their own "relationship templates", as this awareness helps to shed more light on the client's experience and keep it as the focus of the therapy.
11. Ainsworth, M. D. S., & Bell, S. M. (1970). Attachment, exploration, and separation: Illustrated by the behaviour of one-year-olds in a strange situation. *Child Development, 41*: 49–67; Bowlby, J. (1969/1982). Attachment and loss: Vol. 1. *Attachment.* New York: Basic Books.
12. Baldwin, M. W., & Fehr, B. (1995). On the instability of attachment style ratings. *Personal Relationships, 2*(3): 247–261; Cozzarelli, C., Karafa, J. A., Collins, N. L., & Tagler, M. J. (2003). Stability and change in adult attachment styles: Associations with personal vulnerabilities, life events, and global construals of self and others. *Journal of Social and Clinical Psychology, 22*(3): 315–346; Davila, J., Burge, D., & Hammen, C. (1997). Why does attachment change? *Journal of Personality and Social Psychology, 73*(4): 826–838.
13. Tift, B. (2015). *Already Free: Buddhism Meets Psychotherapy on the Path to Liberation.* Colorado: Sounds True.
14. Klein, S. B. (2010). The self: as a construct in psychology and neuropsychological evidence for its multiplicity. *Wiley Interdisciplinary Reviews Cognitive Science, 1*(2): 172–183.

Chapter 5 Identities of superiority

15. It is probably not a coincidence that I suggested to Michael he may have felt inadequate or criticised: two feelings that I had felt in our session together. Had I been able to acknowledge to myself my own experience of these feelings before this point, I probably would have been able to embody a more tender attitude towards him. In a sense, I was disowning, or projecting, my own feelings: a concept we will explore in the next chapter.
16. Crenshaw, K. (1989). Demarginalizing the intersection of race and sex: A black feminist critique of antidiscrimination doctrine. *University of Chicago Legal Forum*, pp. 139–168.

Chapter 6 Becoming divided

17. For an in-depth exploration of the alienation from both our senses and the natural world that has occurred alongside the rise of civilisation, see Abram, D. (1996). *The Spell of the Sensuous: Perception and Language in a More-Than-Human World*. New York: Pantheon Books.
18. This is an attempt to portray how we might collectively perceive our cosmology as a felt experience (in a phenomenological sense), rather than in a scientifically accurate manner.
19. Jung, C. G. (1979). *Aion: Researches into the Phenomenology of the Self*. Princeton, NJ: Princeton University Press.
20. Whilst not all aspects of homophobia can be reduced to the phenomena of projection and psychological defence mechanisms, it is worth noting that more accepting attitudes towards sexuality lead to less inner and outer division, as illustrated in the paper by Weinstein. N., Ryan, W. S., Dehaan, C. R., Przybylski, A. K., Legate, N., & Ryan, R. M. (2012). Parental autonomy support and discrepancies between implicit and explicit sexual identities: Dynamics of self acceptance and defence. *Journal of Personality and Social Psychology*, *102*(4): 815–832.
21. Beard. R. (2021). *Sad Little Men*. London: Harvill Secker.

Chapter 7 The denial of interdependency

22. King, M. L. (1991). A Christmas sermon on peace. In: *A Testament of Hope: The Essential Writings of Martin Luther King, Jr.* James Melvin Washington (Ed.). San Francisco, CA: Harper, p. 253.
23. Gethin, R. (1998). *Foundations of Buddhism*. Oxford: Oxford University Press, p. 141.

24. Nhat Hanh, T. (1992). *Peace in Every Step*. New York: Bantam US.
25. Winnicott, D. W. (1960). The theory of the parent-infant relationship. *International Journal of Psychoanalysis*, 41: 586.
26. Korzybski, A. H. S. (1933). *Science and Sanity: An Introduction to Non-Aristotelian Systems and General Semantics*. New York: International Non-Aristotelian Library, 750.
27. The Holy Bible. Genesis. 3:6–7 (1979) *New International Version*. London: Hodder & Stoughton.
28. Sahn, Seung (1976). *Dropping Ashes on the Buddha: The Teachings of Zen Master Seung Sahn*. New York: Grove Press.

Chapter 8 The return of the exiled

29. Adapted from Ovid (2004). *Ovid Metamorphoses*. R. J. Tarrant (Ed.). Oxford Classical Texts. London: Oxford University Press.
30. This is a combination of both Kohut's and Winnicott's notions of developmental "mirroring". Kohut emphasises the need for our grandiosity to be reflected back to us, whereas Winnicott focuses on the reflection of our emotional experience. Kohut, H. (1971). *The Analysis of the Self*. New York: International Universities Press; Winnicott, D. W. (1971). *Playing & Reality*. London: Tavistock.
31. Williamson, M. (2012). [Twitter] 20 August. https://x.com/marwilliamson/status/237580962219839489 (last accessed 22 September 2024).
32. Freud, S. (1893). Miss Lucy R. In: Studies on Hysteria. *The Standard Edition of the Complete Psychological Works of Sigmund Freud, Volume II (1893–1895)*. London: Hogarth, pp. 106–124.
33. Adapted from Nicholson, R. A. (1925). *The Mathnawī of Jalāl al-Dīn Rūmī*. London: Luzac & Co.
34. For more information on trauma, see Van der Kolk, B. A. (2015). *The Body Keeps the Score: Brain, Mind, and Body in the Healing of Trauma*. New York: Penguin.

Chapter 9 Embracing dependency

35. Oliver, M. (1986). Wild geese. In: *Dream Work*. Boston: Atlantic Monthly Press.
36. For more information on the "frame", see Gray, A. (2014). *An Introduction to the Therapeutic Frame*. Oxfordshire: Routledge.
37. Winnicott, D. W. (1965). *The Maturational Processes and the Facilitating Environment: Studies in the Theory of Emotional Development*. Madison, CT: International Universities Press.

Chapter 10 Discovering our interdependent nature

38. Kafka, F. (2006). *The Zurau Aphorisms*. M. Pasley (Trans.). London: Harvill Secker.
39. This web, or net, is an ancient image from Hindu and Buddhist philosophy that portrays the way in which we are all connected. At each node on the web hangs a jewel that holds within it the reflection of all the other infinite jewels. For more information, see Cook, F. H. (1977). *Hua-Yen Buddhism: The Jewel Net of Indra*. Pennsylvania State Press.
40. Douglas-Klotz, N. (1990). *Prayers of the Cosmos: Reflections on the Original Meaning of Jesus's Words*. New York: HarperOne.
41. Zhuangzi (2013). *The Complete Works of Zhuangzi*. B. Watson (Trans.). New York: Columbia University Press.
42. Rumi, J. al-D. M. (1926). *The Mathnawí of Jalálu'ddín Rúmí: Volume 3*. R. A. Nicholson (Trans.). Cambridge: E. J. W. Gibb Memorial Trust.
43. Hopwood, T. (2020). *Mud & Diamonds: A Shingon Buddhist's Journey*. Uxbridge: Alba Publishing.
44. Blake, W. (2004). *The Complete Poems of William Blake*. A. D. K. M. St. John (Ed.). London: Penguin.

Index